More Praise for *A Live Controversy*

"Courageous and persistent parents have been the force that has transformed public education for children with substantial disabilities. *A Live Controversy*, the story of the Hartmann's decade long struggle to fully include their son Mark in classes with non-disabled students from kindergarten through high school, provides us an in-depth understanding of parent power and the challenges parents like the Hartmanns must confront. But *A Live Controversy* takes us below the surface, beyond winners and losers to an in-depth exploration of all the multi-layered educational, advocacy and legal processes. Much of its instructional value comes from the wise and liberal use of primary source materials that reveal the perspectives and real time thinking of the teachers, experts, lawyers and various school officials. *A Live Controversy* is a rich, comprehensive study with national significance for inclusive education: it is also an inspirational tale of what it takes for parents, schools for all children."
Frank Laski, Esq., Past President, TASH

"A Live Controversy has it all, for the parent, the educator, and the related service provider for children with autism. It is a 'must read' if you work with or represent children with disabilities. It contains incredible detail of events, in a moving, emotional chronological story about Mark and his parents' quest for his inclusion with other students. By reading this book, if you are a parent of a child with autism, you will learn how to help the other 'Marks' out there and avoid the roadblocks and problems encountered by the Hartmanns. If you are an educator, your eyes will be opened to the mistakes, and in some instances, the abuse, perpetrated on the parents. You will learn how to avoid becoming part of the problem, and instead become part of the solution."
Peter W. D. Wright, Esq., co-author *Wrightslaw: Special Education Law*; *Wrightslaw: From Emotions to Advocacy*; *Wrightslaw: No Child Left Behind*. Adjunct Faculty, Special Education Law and Advocacy, William and Mary School of Law

"An amazing story of adversity and victory against impossible odds. Provides much needed inspiration for parents to move ahead in advocacy and to provide a quality of life for all of their children. It is clear these parents deeply love their child."
Thomas McKean, Partner in Policymaking, Colonel, HOKO author, *Soon Will Come the Light: A View From Inside the Autism Puzzel*; author, *Light on the horizon: A Deeper View From Inside the Autism Puzzel*; www.thomasamckean.com

"Inclusion isn't just about including a child with a disability; it is also about including a family. The Hartmanns taught my fellow educators and me lessons from their expertise on Mark, as the two most critically important individuals in Mark's life. It takes a team to include a child."
Kenna M. Colley, Ph.D., Ed.D. Assistant Professor, Radford University

"As an individual with autism, I understand the benefits for students within the Autism Spectrum Disorder (ASD) to have the right to an education that is inclusive. *A Live Controversy* is one such example that strengthens this point: those of us with ASD can achieve great personal successes in educational settings that do not isolate us from neuro-typical society. This is the story of a family who has made a positive impact to the autism community. The emotions enclosed inside are raw, powerful, and driven with no sign of giving in. And the subject material is beautifully executed. *A Live Controversy* is a highly recommended read!"
Lindsey Nebeker, autism advocate/speaker

"Roxana and Joseph Hartmann's personal journey with autism, from the initial diagnosis of their son to their dealings with the educational system, will be an eye-opener for many people, including school administrators and teachers, government officials, medical professionals, and, of course, parents."
Dr. Steve Edelson, Director of the Autism Research Institute, San Diego, California

"A must-read for parents and educators alike. For students of education, it offers all the essential ingredients of a case study on inclusion for a child on the autism spectrum. As parent to a young adult, this book haunted me with the reality of barriers faced in pursuing true inclusion for our son. But the reader will also be reminded that there are people who do grasp the importance of collaboration in addressing individualized needs of students with autism. Kudos to these parents who were trailblazers and had the courage and fortitude to hang in there and tell their story to benefit others."
Lisa A Lieberman, MSW, national speaker and author of *A Stranger Among Us: Hiring In-Home Support for a Child with Autism Spectrum Disorders*

"This book is a straightforward, clearly written account of the experiences of and the lessons learned by Roxana and Joseph Hartmann as they fought for Mark's right to be included in the general education setting—the least restrictive educational environment for him. The Hartmanns share their own story, but it is a story that can speak to other families, friends, and professionals surrounding students with autism

spectrum disorder. This book reflects the best instincts of parents who learned through their own research, reading, trial, and error how best to educate Mark to ensure that he would graduate from high school with a standard diploma—his ticket to more successful post-secondary experiences. Not everyone could separate their family, go through multiple lawsuits, and face the antagonism that Roxana and Joseph did. This book allows others of us invaluable insight into the workings of school divisions and the judicial system. Heartfelt thanks go to Roxana, Joseph, and Mark for the opportunity to learn from their experiences."
Leslie Daniels, Director, T/TAC, Radford University

"Underlying this account of legal wrangling in a climate of mistrust, and amidst almost knee-jerk reactions of school districts to exclude, rather than include, is a remarkable story of a 20-year battle to remove educational barriers, and secure the legal rights for a student to learn and develop to his potential."
Dr. Benjamin Dixon, former Connecticut Deputy Commissioner of Education and Vice President Emeritus, Virginia Tech. Founder/President of Sankofa Futures Consulting, LLC, Blacksburg, Virginia.

"It has been a great privilege to know the Hartmann family for 20 years now! Being a person with autism, I was in special education classes through fourth grade, and their son, Mark Hartmann, was in the same special education program with me in Hampton, Virginia. This was during the late 1980s and the first half of 1990, before I transferred to a regular elementary school in Williamsburg, Virginia. We had a strong family friendship going by that time and still have that friendship going strong today. Through the years, I have witnessed the Hartmanns go through many hurdles in finding the best educational environment for Mark. Joseph has worked at several different locations while Mark was young, and this meant moving from one school system to another. The biggest challenge came to them when they were living in Northern Virginia during the early to mid 1990s. It was very important to them to ensure that Mark received his education in a regular classroom setting, as opposed to a special education classroom where interaction with other peers would be significantly reduced. This book does a great job at explaining how the school system in Northern Virginia failed to meet the needs of the Hartmann family and the legal battle that followed. One of the main goals of this book is to explain the importance of inclusion for people with disabilities, including autism, in a regular classroom setting, and how it has been proven to work!"
Dave Hamrick, meteorologist; weatheringautism@aol.com

"As I read the page proofs for *A Live Controversy*, my first reaction was utter disappointment that I could not have the finished product TODAY to assign to graduate students, give to families, and share with administrators. This is a landmark book about a landmark case; it contains not only the Hartmann's journey to inclusive schooling but many kernels of wisdom that others can use in their own quest for quality education. Parents often tell me, 'I believe in inclusion for my child. I want inclusion for my child. I just don't know how to get inclusion for my child!' Now, I will be able to point these families to *A Live Controversy*. The Hartmann's story may not be typical, but every family will be able to learn from the tenacity, creativity, and vision of these parents and their pioneering son."

Paula Kluth, Ph.D., author of *You're Going to Love This Kid: Teaching Students with Autism in the Inclusive Classroom* and *A Land We Can Share: Teaching Literacy to Students with Autism*

"People have been telling stories since the dawn of time. It is how we learn and create our cultures. Some stories entertain, others teach, and some challenge. This is an important story about our culture—and how much we have still to learn. It is unusual for a family to have the capacity to 'tell it all,' but that is why this is important. They have laid bare their struggle to achieve basic human rights for Mark, when many fought to exclude him. Mark's struggle will be lifelong, but partly because of these pioneering advocates for full citizenship, the lives of others are and will be less painful. And, Mark is clear that his family is with him on this journey, which at this stage is beginning to show rewards for the decades of intense pain, struggle and love."

Jack Pearpoint, Inclusion Press

"As expert witness for the Hartmann family in the Virginia Federal Courtroom of Leonie Brinkema, I can personally attest to incredible adventure they took with amazing belief, tenacity and conviction! After personally observing Mark being educated successfully and thriving in his Blacksburg inclusive classroom, it was clear that he was truly in the least restrictive environment, the general education classroom. We prevailed in this courtroom which was notable considering the judge has a son with Down Syndrome (as an attribute) who had been educated in a self-contained classroom during his school career. This book is essential reading for all educators to understand many important areas, including what an inclusive education should mean, how it is truly possible and how school districts can operate under a model of innovation, support, and possibility rather than fear and protection of outdated, non-student centered models. This book will be required reading for my university students."

Patrick Schwarz, Ph.D., Professor, Diversity in Learning and Teaching Department, National-Louis University, Chicago, Illinois; www.patrickschwarz.com

"Roxana and Joseph Hartmann received the gift of a child that required all of their love and attention, and with incredible courage fought to ensure that he had the same opportunity that all children deserve to develop to his fullest potential. *A Live Controversy* teaches us how to defend the rights of our children and to never give up in the face of prejudice. Their story and their sacrifice for the well-being of their child should serve as a lesson and an inspiration to us all."
Jose Zaglul Sloan, Ph.D., Rector, E.A.R.T.H. University, Costa Rica

"Inclusive schools are where all staff members believe that it is their responsibility to support all students in their learning. The Hartmann's story shows the value of educators and parents working together to support students in a school community."
Martha Ann Stallings, third grade teacher in the 1992 short documentary *Educating Peter*

"All parents of children with disabilities should read this book for three important reasons. First, because they will realize that it is fair, reasonable and better if their children receive individually appropriate educational and related services in integrated settings. Second, because far too many segregationists still determine that their children will function in settings that prevent them from learning to live, work and play effectively in integrated society at school exit. Third, they will realize that integration is worth fighting for and that every demonstration of successful integration is another nail in the coffin of segregation."
Lou Brown, Ph.D., Professor Emeritus, College of Education, University of Wisconsin

"The day will come when it is obvious to everyone that children who experience disabilities belong in their neighborhood schools, educated in the same classrooms as kids who are 'typical' in their development. The separate classrooms so widespread today will be viewed as relics of an uninformed and unimaginative past. One day, educators will argue about the best ways to include all children, rather than argue about whether all children should be included. In the meantime, while history is righting itself, we can learn a great deal from pioneers like Roxana and Joseph Hartmann and their son Mark. What you will find here is a careful and objective rendering of their journey. It is packed with news you can use, a road map for those

who find themselves fighting the philosophical opponents of inclusion."
David Pitonyak, Ph.D., Director of Imagine; www.dimagine.com

"For several years, Joe and Roxana Hartmann and more recently, Mark, have been guest lecturers in one of my classes to provide a family perspective of their journey in educating Mark. Their presentations have been thought provoking and have provided balance to our conversations about ethical decision-making regarding justice and care. This book allows them to share their views on interactions with school districts as seen through the eyes of a family. It has promise of being a valuable tool—for students in education at all levels to assist in understanding the rights of parents in pursuing what they perceive to be an appropriate education for their child."
Brenda Williams, Ph.D., Department of Education, College of William and Mary

"*A Live Controversy* is a story of emergence. It documents one student's progress, then triumph, followed by banishment, only to be then followed by revival and triumph again. While pessimistic educators and lawyers thrash about for how to explain their exclusion of Mark Hartmann from regular public school academics, Mark, his family, and their allies march forward, finding creative ways for Mark to blossom as a student. In a richly told narrative that stretches all the way to the United States Supreme Court, this book encapsulates a national struggle over educational opportunity for students with autism and other developmental disabilities in the dramatic story of one student, Mark Hartmann, and his determined parents. *A Live Controversy* celebrates education as the gateway to full citizenship."
Douglas Biklen, Ph.D., Dean, School of Education, Syracuse University

"This astonishing book is not only part of the history of the disabilities rights movement; for many families, it still reflects present reality. Anyone who cares about the education of diverse learners in our schools—and that should be all of us—will want to know about the Hartmann family's long struggle to secure the inclusion of their son, Mark, in the general curriculum with his peers. Mark's family spoke truth to power at great personal price; their story is an enduring reminder of what families and children with disabilities value most, and an uncomfortable reminder of how far we still have to go."
Pat Amos, M.A., parent advocate, past president of the Autism National Committee; TASH board member.

"A Live Controversy is a journey relived by the parents of Mark Hartmann. Roxana and Joseph Hartmann never refused to give up on their son who was diagnosed with autism. Once Roxana found out about Mark's autism, she reacted to the 'straightforward, clean and unambiguous' diagnosis with fear of the unknown, but later, with a realistic approach—thanking the doctor for her frankness. Many parents can identify with this moment. Roxana stayed focused on Mark by being involved with his schools, volunteering in his classrooms, trying to find and make suitable classroom environments, and finally seeing Mark's progress. They never hesitated—even to go through legal battles for Mark. The book is filled with Mark's wonderful philosophical insights, his family's challenges and detailed descriptions of the IEP process. It is a very useful guidebook for any parent who wishes to see success in their children with autism."
Soma Mukhopadhyay, mother of Tito Mukhopadhyay, Director of Education of Helping Autism Through Learning and Outreach (HALO), Austin, Texas

A LIVE CONTROVERSY

A LIVE CONTROVERSY

*A Story of Autism
and a Family's Determination*

By Roxana and Joseph Hartmann

Brandylane Publishers, Inc.

ISBN 978-1-883911-85-0

Library of Congress Control Number 2009924855

Brandylane Publishers, Inc.
Richmond, Virginia
www.brandylanepublishers.com

To our loving children,
Laura Alexandra and Mark Andrew

Contents

Preface

The story you are about to read is the true story of a family dealing with autism and all that it implies, especially the effects of autism at home and within the public school system. You will read about stress on family life and real challenges related to unwanted behaviors, nonverbal communication, special education programs, the least restrictive environment, and due process. The authors wrote this story in an objective and unabridged manner in hopes that it will serve as a helpful guide of lessons learned, especially beneficial for parents and educators coping with similar circumstances. Finally, the authors are hopeful that it will inspire other parents and educators to become actively engaged in advocating for their own children.

This is also the story of Mark Hartmann, the authors' son, who turned 23 years old on August 21, 2008. Despite the challenges posed by his autism, in 2007, Mark finished his senior year at Blacksburg High School in Blacksburg, Virginia, earning credits for a regular high school diploma. From the beginning of his education to the present, there have been more than eighty professionals working in the field of public education who have interacted with Mark with varying degrees of success. Some of these, including speech therapists, occupational therapists, school administrators, teachers, and special education experts, have been particularly effective and instrumental in helping Mark realize his potential. Unfortunately, others were not committed to inclusion in the public school system and used their time with Mark to justify their own bias against his inclusion in regular-education classrooms.

This is the true story of a five-year legal battle that erupted between the Hartmanns and a public school system over whether Mark could best be educated by being fully included in regular classrooms with non-disabled peers, or whether he would be better served by being segregated in special education programs for children with special needs. Because of the numbers of people who have interacted with Mark during his public education, only those educational professionals who were part of the legal proceedings are mentioned by name, some by ficticious name, in this book. As written in the pages that follow, their relationship to Mark is part of the public record.

Parents reading this book will come to understand the lessons learned by the Hartmanns as they fought for Mark's rights to be included in the least restrictive educational environment. Educators will gain insight into educational philosophies and administrative procedures that may at times conflict with applicable law, especially with the Individuals with Disabilities Education Act (IDEA). In the end, it is the responsibility of those educators to uphold the public's trust and to ensure that *all* children are given a fair and unbiased opportunity to be educated alongside their peers. Parents, educators and other sympathetic readers will come to understand key elements that contributed to Mark's overall success in fully included educational environments throughout his school years. The authors anticipate that these key elements will provide a framework that can benefit other children with autism, the families who love them, and the educators and communities who support them.

Students, educators, legal professionals, parents and others may access original documents, exhibits used in court, videos and photos of Mark at school and home, newspaper articles, videos of appearances on national TV programs, and other information on the Hartmann's website at www.alivecontroversy.com

Acknowledgments

All parents try hard to save money to buy a house and to send their children to college. The reality is that parents do not save money to defend their children from school systems who enforce the status quo. On the other hand, school districts have a budget, in some cases hundreds of thousands of dollars, set aside for their legal fund and to pay retainers to elite law firms, whose staff is ready to represent the district in an instant. Most lawyers who specialize in special education law, work for these elite firms. There are very few lawyers who choose to practice law to help families with children with disabilities, and subsequently, to represent the family's beliefs and their quest for equality and justice. We have great respect and admiration for Gerard 'Jerry' S. Rugel, the attorney who represented us, and his wife Anne, who were loyal to Mark and understanding of our commitment to full inclusion. Jerry became family to us during the five years of the legal process, as he represented our position and fought tirelessly and competently for Mark's educational rights. Jerry will always be in our thoughts.

Our expert witnesses made all the difference in the world during court testimony in describing Mark's performance in a well-managed and executed inclusion program during fourth grade in Montgomery County, Virginia. Their testimony contrasted sharply with what had happened to Mark during second grade in Loudoun County. Dr. Patrick Anthony Schwarz, Dr. Kenna Cooley, Beverly Strager, and Gregory Paynter, all valued friends and professionals, were persuasive witnesses in federal court and were key in winning the actual litigation in our legal fight. In addition, we recognize the support that all of the special education and regular education teachers at Kipps Elementary School, including the principal, Dr. Ray Van Dyke, provided to Mark. These teachers all were committed and dedicated to the idea that *all children are valued for who they are*. Sharing this same belief were our friends from Butterfield School in Lombard, Illinois, Sandra 'Sandy' K. Truax, the principal, and Mary Ann Mrazek, Mark's first grade aide, who also testified on Mark's behalf.

Other experts in education also supported us during the Due Process Hearing: Anne Malatchi and Audrey Russo traveled far to support us without expecting anything in return. To them, the cause was reason enough—a child in jeopardy. Cathy A. Thornton, Mark's tutor during the time he needed support and love, helped us to renew our faith in special education professionals.

Our loyal friend, Jamie Ruppmann, a wonderful advocate for special education at the national level, joined us to interview lawyers when we knew that Loudoun County Public Schools was getting ready to file a Due Process claim against us. We learned with Jamie that lawyers are like shoes … they come in all sizes and colors. And we came to the realization that many lawyers do not care about commitment or the facts of the case. As one lawyer put it, "It's about money." Jamie, with her expertise after many years in the field of advocacy for families and children in the autism spectrum, does not see any boundaries in education.

During the time when "inclusion" was not a part of the Individuals with Disabilities Education Act (IDEA), Judith Heumann, the Assistant Secretary of Education in the Office of Special Education and Rehabilitation Services under the Clinton Administration, reached out to us to offer her support. When the Fourth Circuit Court of Appeals overturned and remanded the federal court's decision in our case, Ms. Heumann called us and invited us to a meeting in her office to review the legal issues we faced. The legal team assembled by Ms. Heumann was truly impressive. It included a group of lawyers from the Department of Justice who were reviewing our case to prepare an *amicus curie* brief on our behalf … if we decided to take our case to the U.S. Supreme Court. The group included Acting Assistant Attorney General, Mark L. Gross, Michelle M. Aronowitz, U.S. Department of Justice, Judith A. Winston, General Counsel, and Francisco Lopez, Department of Education. The commitment of this team of legal advocates—all public servants who openly stand beside parents—was truly heart warming to us. Without them, our educational laws would be weak and would not support parents and children.

We would never have been able to continue our legal battle without the support of The Association of Severely Handicapped (TASH). Mr. Frank Laski, President of TASH and at the time the attorney who represented the Oberti case in New Jersey, secured for us Dr. Schwarz, our expert witness for the federal court bench trial. We are also indebted to the Autism National Committee for its focus on protecting the civil rights of people in the autism spectrum. We also recognize Dr. Douglas Biklen, Director of the Facilitated Communication Institute at Syracuse University. Dr. Biklen and his talented staff are committed to bringing an effective augmentative communication method to people around the world who are nonverbal.

We want to acknowledge our friends, Robert and Eleanor Voldish, who stood by us throughout the legal ordeal. When we were new to the community in Loudoun County, they organized events where parents and advocates could share their frustrations with a school system resistant to change. To Rita Lewis for your support and advocacy, and to our very special friends, Lisa and Gregg Robinson, who were there offering a helping hand at a time when we really needed friends, we are forever grateful.

Then there are the parents of children with disabilities we met along our journey. These are very special people: Sue Moreno, for sharing her story of Beth; Tommy and Sylvia Tsoutsoures and their son Pierce; William and Phyllis Plekavic and their twins Scott and Clint; Gail and Dick Blogg and their son Malcolm and Janel Williams and her son Lance. They always were ready to listen and to provide support to continue this journey in Chicago; and, our dear friend Cindy Hamrick and her son David

Hamrick—we have shared so much. You both deserve our special thanks. We also want to recognize Sue Swedly, who volunteered as Mark's aide for an entire year without pay, and Betty Thompson and her son Matt, for coming to our rescue when we needed someone to care for Mark and Laura while we went to court. Our good friend Elin Doval and Robert—you have a very special place in our hearts.

We want to thank the many professionals working on issues related to the autism spectrum: Dr. Luke Tsai of the University of Michigan and Dr. Edwin Cook of the University of Chicago—thank you for teaching parents about drugs and their side effects, and about your research in medications for people with autism. Your insights brought resolve into our life to raise Mark without resorting to any medications. That alone is priceless.

Our journey and vision for Mark would not have taken place without the PATH and MAAPs process. Thank you Jack Pearpoint, Marsha Forest, and John O'Brien for the development of these tools. The concept of inclusion for Mark came from the positive results of the research conducted by Dr. Anne Donnellan of the University of Wisconsin. Dr. Donnellan's presentation at the ASA National Conference in Indianapolis during July 1991 was truly inspiring for us. Through the years, we have valued being in touch and sharing Mark's progress.

We continue to learn and meet new people along our journey. We want to acknowledge HALO (Helping Autism through Learning and Outreach) in Austin, Texas. To Linda Lange, founder and president of HALO, your vision to bring Soma Mukhopadhyay, the pioneer in RPM (Rapid Response Method), another alternative augmentative communication system, along with her son, Tito to Austin, Texas to be the Director of Education for HALO, was truly inspirational. HALO's work has benefited hundreds of children around the world. We are confident that RPM will bring a brighter future for all children with limited communication skills.

Finally … our families: to Laura for her insight in suggesting the title for this book; to Joseph's parents, George F. and Anna Marie Hartmann for their advocacy for my sister Veronica "Ronny" in the 1950s when children with disabilities did not have access to public schools. With their hard work in fundraising and organizing, they created a program for children with disabilities in the basement of a church—the beginning of the disability rights movement in Illinois. My sister, Mariana, brother George F., his wife Sharon and brother Paul, our deepest love and gratitude for your unending support. To Roxana's parents in Costa Rica … Sigifredo Villalta and Teresa Sanchez; to her brothers, Omar, Sergio, Sigifredo, Mauricio, Gustavo, Luis, and to her sisters, Grace, Lidia, Aida, Teresita, Maria Elena, our deepest love and gratitude.

To our community of friends in Blacksburg who provide Mark with a place where he is loved and welcomed … you know who you are … thank you. To our friends overseas and those with whom we served in our career in the Foreign Service around the globe, we will always cherish your inspiration and undying support.

Finally, our deep appreciation to all those who managed this book through the publishing process, especially to Robert Pruett, our talented publisher; and to Tanya Griffith, who shaped and honed our work with loving expertise.

CHAPTER 1

BETRAYAL OF TRUST
1994

Before entering the meeting room, the vice principal stopped us in the hall and told us that there would be a forty-five-minute time limit for this IEP meeting (Individualized Education Plan) and that he would be the timekeeper. *That's strange,* Joseph thought. *There had never been a time limit even mentioned before.*

But this was not the first troubling sign of a hidden agenda in our relationship with the staff at Ashburn Elementary School in Loudoun County, Virginia. Just weeks before, following a truly contentious IEP meeting on March 18, 1994, we wrote a personal letter to Ms. Meadows, the principal at Ashburn E.S. We wanted to ensure that she understood what "the process" had become. More importantly, we also wanted to reassure her that, in spite of disagreements and difficulties, we were still fully committed to cooperating and working with the school staff to improve Mark's educational program. Moreover, the letter reflected our heightened emotional state and near-panic that something was terribly wrong. We felt that we had to reach out for understanding, if nothing else. The letter read:

> It was with trepidation that we began working with the staff at Ashburn E.S. We focused most on the fact that Mark was going to be the first child with autism included in the regular classroom setting at the school. Having experienced this same anxiety in Illinois, we were painfully aware of the pitfalls to any school system and teaching staff.
>
> We also knew that if support for the staff was not provided early in the inclusion process through special education resources and through other services, it would be a frustrating experience for all involved. This could easily lead to the conclusion that "it just doesn't work, despite our best efforts." After all, Mark was a unique child

in an inclusive placement, a new experience for the staff at Ashburn E.S.

As parents on the sidelines, we watched as the frustration grew over time. It was apparent to us that the staff was not getting the kind of support and guidance that it needed. Without fault, Ms. Kelly (the able Director of Special Education in Loudoun County) functioned more in the role of an administrator than as a knowledgeable guide to the staff. From our perspective, the staff lacked the effective support of an inclusion coordinator, which was undermining their concerted efforts and threatening the success of Mark's inclusion program. Our hearts were being slowly torn out day by day as we witnessed the staff's frustration in working with Mark, all for lack of proper guidance.

One major event shocked us into the realization that something had to be done quickly in order to salvage the best out of the circumstances that had developed. This event was a call from Mr. Dotson (the vice principal at Ashburn E.S.) asking Roxana to come to school to pick-up Mark and take him home. We had never been faced with this situation before, and we realized that we were facing a serious indicator of probable failure, if things don't change. In fact, there were two victims here, the school staff and Mark, both for the same reason, a lack of appropriate and effective support.

Finally, the issue of trust (our trust) in the staff was cast in doubt during the meeting on March 18th. Frankly, we can only say that we entrust the staff implicitly with the responsibility to provide the best that they can for Mark during his hours at school, day by day.

Past cases and experiences cry out to us in a loud voice warning us as parents of a handicapped child, "do not be taken in, know your rights and insist that the school system respects them." Imagine the fear that flows through us when Mark's placement in an inclusion program for next year is brought into question and opened for debate. Imagine the fear that flows through us when our request for a planning session to discuss Mark's program for this summer, and preparations for next year, is dismissed quickly as perhaps not being necessary.

Please understand that these concerns are not with the staff at Ashburn E.S. Rather, they are with the school administrators in Loudoun County (such as Mr. Neil Winters), who have remained in the shadows during the year and may not be convinced that inclusion is a valid method to teach children who are as capable of learning as Mark is.

We never received a response to our letter from Ms. Meadows, nor even a comment to acknowledge it. Her non-response appeared to be a concrete symbol of Loudoun County Public School's (LCPS) attitude toward us. We had become the enemy in an undeclared war over the inclusion of a nine-year-old, second-grade boy with autism—but we didn't recognize it. Naivety blocked the truth. We simply believed too much in everyone's goodness that we couldn't imagine that LCPS would be pitted against us in a strategy to dominate Mark's education in a way we opposed.

Now we were at the final IEP meeting of the year to chart Mark's third grade program for the upcoming 1994-95 school year. The meeting had been set for May 31st. We had no way of knowing that it was to be an excruciating and painful experience for us, as parents.

There had never before been a fixed time limit set for any meeting with the Ashburn E.S. staff, but today, we had just forty-five minutes. Mark's second grade teacher, Ms. Jarrett, the school's speech pathologist, Ms. Conroy-Winters, and the special education teacher, Ms. Mason, each submitted her annual report of Mark's performance during the year, and then one by one, read her recommendation from a prepared statement.

Any observer would have known instantly that heightened emotions filled the room, yet as the staff read their reports, we weren't immediately alarmed. Much of Mark's performance outlined in these new reports hadn't changed from the facts and anecdotal information presented earlier at the March 18th IEP meeting. One new element jumped out at us; however, Ms. Mason was named on these documents as being Mark's "case manager." Throughout the year, Ms. Conroy-Winters had always been Mark's case manager, and we were never advised of any change. Something seemed amiss; this small detail appeared out of place.

Following the submission of the annual reports, each staff member was asked to make recommendations regarding Mark's third grade education at Ashburn E.S., 1994-95. Ms. Jarrett was the first to read her statement:

> Academically, Mark has shown no growth. In looking back on Mark's behavior charts, I notice that Mark's aggressive behavior increased when new concepts were introduced. Academically, Mark has not benefited in the classroom or in whole group or cooperative group settings. Mark has shown the most success when he is working one-on-one with a familiar adult. Mark needs to learn life skills and most importantly, communication skills. The progress I have seen Mark make on his communication board demonstrates that working with Mark more on a one-to-one basis will be a great deal

more successful for him. Because of Mark's desire for many breaks, many snacks and little work, he has had a lot of "down time" in the classroom. Mark has shown extreme aggressive behavior to adults working with him and the children in the classroom. At times, this has been a dangerous situation for the other students. As Mark grows and becomes stronger, it is more difficult to stop this behavior. I fear in time a student or adult could get seriously hurt. Mark's voice sounds have gotten louder as the year progressed. As a result, he has distracted the other students and made it difficult for them to pay attention to what they are being taught. It is my professional opinion that we are doing a great disservice to Mark to include him in a regular third-grade classroom next year. This would not be an appropriate placement for Mark to learn the skills he will need to learn.

We fell into absolute shock after Ms. Jarrett read her statement! With a grim face and holding emotions in check, Joseph told the assemblage in a voice of controlled rage, "What you intend to do, to change Mark's placement to a segregated program, is our worst possible nightmare! How dare you use your positions as teachers of children to conspire against us like this? This IEP meeting is obviously a set up, concocted by you all, all traitors to the truth and disguised as educational professionals. Why didn't even one of you communicate your concerns over Mark's placement to us before this? Even though this evil – your intent – is shocking to us, get on with it. I want to hear what else you all have to say."

The attitude and demeanor of the staff appeared self-righteous, defiant, arrogant and uncompromising as they continued, always framing their comments in the context of doing what was best for Mark. We resented this greatly but were powerless to stop the assault. Roxana began weeping uncontrollably and could not regain her composure. She was forced to leave the meeting. Joseph stayed the course with Mrs. Jamie Ruppmann, an educational advocate who was helping us, to hear the statements from the rest of the Ashburn E.S. staff.

Ms. Conroy-Winters spoke next:

Mark does not appear to benefit from being in a regular class. He has shown some ability to learn to communicate independently in a smaller, more structured environment. Because his communication needs are so great, I feel his current, fully included setting is clearly inappropriate and I cannot recommend that he continue in this placement any longer. I do feel that Mark will regress over the summer in his communication skills due to lack of practice. Therefore, I recommend that he continue to receive one hour per day of speech/language services for the extended school year. My feeling is that four weeks of speech/language therapy would be appropriate.

As they read their statements, Joseph noticed that both Ms. Jarrett's and Ms. Conroy-Winters' statements appeared to be cutouts from the same document. Comparing them later, we found that the type was the same, the margins were the same, and the commas were hardly visible in both. LCPS obviously had planned carefully for this IEP meeting. We suspect that everything said was approved in advance by the LCPS central office, if not directly by its attorney.

We came to believe that the attorney for LCPS, Kathleen Shepherd Mehfoud of Richmond, Virginia had been providing guidance to the Ashburn E.S. staff, indirectly through the supervisors and administrators at the LCPS central office, beginning as early as November 1993. Undoubtedly, her purpose was to chart a legal strategy for LCPS on how to build a compelling case against Mark's continued inclusion at Ashburn E.S. that would result in his removal from the regular classroom and placement in a segregated special education program. Such intent severely compromised the IEP team's ability to freely develop and implement an individualized educational program for Mark that would address his many needs, given their unspoken agenda.

Things became much clearer once the school system's purpose was exposed. After all, school officials were not calling Ms. Mehfoud for advice on how to improve Mark's educational program, but rather for legal advice on how to circumvent Mark's academic inclusion. Based on its actions and inactions throughout the school year, undoubtedly, LCPS had been plotting against us.

Ms. Mason's statement during the IEP meeting was hand written and entitled, "Placement Recommendation, 1994-95." Ms. Mason wrote:

> Mark is a youngster who exhibits significant deficits in cognitive, communication, social and adaptive behavior skills. Mark's learning style and curriculum goals are qualitatively different from his classmates. Using an adapted regular classroom curriculum with Mark does not provide an educational program with the scope, sequence and unique elements that Mark requires. A program of inclusion in the regular classroom does not appear to be appropriate to meet Mark's educational needs.

Surprisingly, Joseph did not disagree with Ms. Mason's portrayal of Mark's deficits, only with her approach on how to best address them. In effect, Ms. Mason was saying: Mark is a boy with autism whose learning style is different from his typical peers; therefore, he should not be in a regular classroom. Stereotypical approaches such as hers appeared to justify the segregation of literally all children with disabilities from their peers in public education.

The IEP team members from Loudoun County Public Schools unanimously recommended that Mark attend a segregated classroom for children with autism at Leesburg Elementary School for his third-grade year. We couldn't help but feel betrayed, abused, and violated by each and every person on the side of LCPS! The weeks and months of frustration with Mark's inclusion program appeared to be part of the overall plan to build a case for segregating our son at school. After it was all spilled onto the table, Joseph refused to sign the proposed IEP for Mark. We were now confronting the status quo in Loudoun County, about to become embroiled in a fierce battle between the principles of tradition versus educational change.

While the year at Ashburn E.S. had been a hard one, our prior challenges and successes fortified and prepared us for the fight ahead. Given our refusal to support the proposed IEP, LCPS's next step was to take legal action against us to obtain the authority to move Mark to the segregated autism program against our wishes. It didn't take LCPS long to act.

CHAPTER 2

DIAGNOSIS AUTISM - 1988

The neurologist walked into the waiting room with a sullen face. He began by apologizing for what he was about to say and then leveled with us: evaluation results indicated that Mark had a severe speech development delay with autistic characteristics—and that, unfortunately, there was nothing they could do for him.

As he continued, Roxana felt her heart racing. Even though we had prepared ourselves for this news, tears filled our eyes as we tried to focus on the meaning of the doctor's words. We couldn't immediately respond.

Without asking, the doctor continued. He told us that if Mark were to recover his ability to talk, it would likely be within the next five years or so, perhaps earlier. He added that it becomes less likely after a child turns eight. Contradicting an earlier hearing test that indicated that Mark was nearly deaf in one ear, the neurologist commented that Mark definitely did *not* have any hearing loss in either ear. He concluded that hearing was not a factor in Mark's lack of speech development over the past three months and that the initial hearing test must have been flawed.

It had been just over three months since we had first consulted with the pediatric neurologist. We became concerned when Mark stopped using words and phrases to express his needs. He also appeared somewhat withdrawn at home, especially when playing with his older sister, Laura. Mark was not even noticing when Joseph returned home from work. Previously, this was a high point in his day, one that would bring him running and shouting, "Daddy, Daddy, Daddy!" Without speculating on any diagnosis at that first consultation, the neurologist had recommended that Mark needed a concentrated regimen of speech therapy and extended time with his playgroup. Finally, he had recommended that we have Mark's hearing tested.

The hearing test indicated that Mark was deaf in the right ear and sixty percent deaf in the left ear. That news made us sick with worry for our little boy, then just twenty-seven months.

The three months following our initial consultation passed quickly and, in January 1988, the neurologist recommended placing Mark in the Medical College of Virginia for testing to determine if brain maladies were causing Mark's developmental decline. During his four-day stay in the hospital, Mark received an MRI, an EEG and a complete battery of blood tests, hearing tests and neurological tests, as well as psychiatric and developmental evaluations. Roxana stayed with Mark at the hospital to comfort him through the ordeal. He was just two-and-a-half years old.

Our son had been born normally and without incident. Thus, it was hard for us to accept the fact that our healthy little boy was regressing developmentally and that there was nothing that we could do about it. It was like living through a nightmare.

Diagnosis Confirmed

The pediatric neurologist was careful not to shock us with his diagnosis. Following discussions that elaborated the results of the medical tests and evaluations, he recommended that we seek a second opinion and gave us the name of a prominent neurologist in the field of autism research at the Albert Einstein Medical Center in New York, Dr. Isabelle Rapin.

Within days, we had an appointment at the center. Roxana and Mark flew to New York and were met by Lisa Robinson, a family friend who lived there. Despite having Lisa there to help Roxana, it was a very difficult trip. On the day of the appointment, New York experienced a nine-inch snowstorm and much of the city was snowed in. That did not deter Roxana, however. Lisa, Roxana and Mark arrived at the center on time for the appointment.

The doctor, an experienced medical professional who had dedicated her life's work to autism research, examined Mark and spent time with him observing how he reacted to various stimuli in the play area. Following the evaluation, she called Roxana into her office.

Dr. Rapin looked at Roxana with motherly eyes and said, simply, that Mark was a child with autism. After a long moment of silence, she advised Roxana to take Mark home and be good to him. As the doctor reviewed the basis for her conclusions, fear and anxiety overwhelmed Roxana and pierced her heart. This time, the diagnosis was straightforward, clean and unambiguous! While shaken by the doctor's candor, Roxana was more frightened of the unknown, of what lay ahead.

During the short time they were together, Dr. Rapin tried to console and support Roxana. She told Roxana that she didn't have a crystal ball, but that with patience and the right therapies, Mark could have a good life. She told Roxana that it was important for her to hold onto her dreams and expectations for Mark, because those dreams could make all the difference. After composing herself, Roxana thanked the doctor for her frankness. Nonetheless, she felt bewildered; there was no specific advice on what we should do next.

About Autism

Both of us were worried and scared beyond words, not knowing a thing about autism or what Mark's prognosis would be. We began seeking information on autism and read everything available on the developmental disability, searching for answers. We found clues about the reality of Mark's future, but not much hope.

From our research, we learned that autism is defined as a neurological disorder that results in a life-long developmental disability, primarily affecting a person's communication skills, social awareness, and behavior. Its symptoms impact human behavior to varying degrees, but can affect movement, attention, learning, memory, language, mood and social interaction. Specific behavior patterns were found to vary widely from one individual to another. Overall, children with autism are taxed by typical social interactions, experience receptive/expressive communication delays affecting both their understanding and use of language, and respond unusually to sensory stimuli. Despite these challenges, many children with autism are of average intelligence. A significant percentage is well above average, and many are brilliant.

We learned that children with autism appear to withdraw into a world of their own and oftentimes remain socially isolated. In many cases, these children may lose their ability to effectively share their feelings, thoughts, fears, hopes, and even their words with others. Children with autism demonstrate a resistance to change and insist upon routines. They appear to rely upon structure and routine to maintain their comfort level and are easily upset if that structure or routine is changed. Children with autism sometimes express their heightened stress level through behavioral outbursts, which, unfortunately, may cause tension for those around them.

Learning the "how" and "why" of autism was not easy for us, nor was there much concrete information available at that time. What was evident was there was no cure for autism. Pouring over research for answers, we finally concluded that, in great measure, autism remained a mystery to the medical profession! Even though we tried to use Mark's pediatric doctor as a resource for information on autism, it was hopeless. Then it hit us: Pediatricians focus on childhood diseases and illness…vomiting and diarrhea…not on developmental disorders and how to treat them. This realization changed our thinking dramatically! In fact, most of the really helpful information about how to deal with autism came from our own research and from other parents. We became nearly obsessed with seeking out the latest information, conferences, workshops, and anything else that would provide constructive guidance on how to work with Mark and what we should be doing.

After digesting all of the popular theories that have been promulgated, we suspect that Mark's autism most likely stems from a genetic weakness or unknown susceptibility, coupled with other unknown environmental factors. Of concern were Mark's childhood vaccinations and the overuse of antibiotics for ear infections. Together, we judge that these circumstances, perhaps coupled with other factors, interfered with the normal development of Mark's brain at a critical time when he was a toddler. Therefore, we were given the label of "Infantile Autism" to describe Mark's developmental disability (Author's note: Infantile Autism was later reclassified under DSM-IV as Childhood Disintegrative Disorder).

What to do? How to cope?

Nonetheless, a speech therapist recommended that early intervention with an array of therapies was critically important to diminish the severity of the disorder. While we continued to acquire knowledge about autism, Roxana followed this advice by contacting the Child Developmental Resources (CDR) in Williamsburg, Virginia, to obtain sensory integration therapy and speech therapy for Mark.

We continued the playgroup activities to help Mark socially, as well as to strengthen his motor skills. We also put Mark outside with Laura to run and play with all the neighborhood toddlers and preschoolers. We tried to make it fun for all of the children and devoted time to planning special activities for them. We often went to big playgrounds together and ate out at McDonald's. The other moms pitched in as well. Our house became Grand Central Station, where all were welcomed. We wanted Mark to become closely associated with his peers and to model them through parallel play. We all had a good time together!

We soon realized that Mark had strengths in visual acuity whereby he could recognize differences in the shapes of objects and in sequencing. He was a master at putting together puzzles as large as 100 pieces by the time he was four! He could recognize a needed piece even though it was laying face down on the table. We tried to cope with the limitations brought on by Mark's autism while celebrating the strengths evident in our young son, all the while trying to keep our lives as normal as possible.

As parents, we coped by staying focused on doing everything we could do to meet Mark's needs. We even adjusted his diet early on, after we found out that many children have autistic-like symptoms brought on by allergies to certain foods, especially wheat products and milk. We followed prudent dietary guidelines, put him on a milk-free diet, and restricted Mark from all foods/products that had yeast or artificial colorants. We noticed mild changes in Mark, but nothing significant. On balance though, he became less anxious and more focused. Curiously, neither of us considered medication as a remedy for Mark's unwanted behaviors.

Nevertheless, our insecurity and lack of knowledge about autism caused us continual worry. To lose one's healthy little boy is unimaginable, but it happened. Over the span of weeks, our happy, affectionate son had drifted away. Mark's very being no longer seemed to be with us, yet with ironic ambiguity, his physical presence was left behind. This realization hit us hard. We couldn't help but grieve for Mark and looked to each other and to God for solace. Yet while we grieved for the loss of our son on many levels, we simply had no time or energy for rage, denial, pity or anger.

Unfortunately, the rest of our world simply couldn't appreciate what we faced. It was comparable to a child dying, but there was no funeral. Our friends told us, "Well, you're just having problems with your kid; he'll get over it." No one really understood the magnitude of the crisis we faced, nor the pain we suffered over the fact that Mark would *not* "get over it." Concerning our emotional well-being, we tried to be pragmatic and to accept our roles as parents of a child with autism. We tried to use common sense in making plans and decisions, and focused on Mark's needs, his overall health and well-being.

Through it all, though, we felt isolated because we were unable to connect with other parents who faced the same problems we did. This was the dark ages before the Internet, and there was no easy way to connect with people who had children with autism. At times, we cried and felt depressed. The sparkle of hope that someday Mark would overcome this gradually faded away. In the end, we only hoped Mark would survive autism intact and become reasonably self-sufficient as an adult.

CHAPTER 3

EARLY INTERVENTION
1988-1990

"We plan for Mark to stay in your special education program until he turns five," Roxana said to the teacher. "Then, we'll start him in kindergarten." The teacher looked at Roxana in disbelief as she took Mark by the hand to lead him into the classroom. The teacher then remarked that she thought Roxana was being overly optimistic, adding that Mark may *never* be able to be in a regular classroom. Stopping to lecture Roxana about Mark's disability, the teacher basically said that Mark's learning capacity was *severely* impaired and, while a wonderful little boy, she predicted that his behaviors would only get worse as he grew older. While Roxana knew that the teacher was only speaking from her own experience, for Roxana, her underlying message of hopelessness was just flatly unthinkable!

Besides our concerns about Mark's developmental disability, we faced an educational system filled with teachers, administrators, and professionals who, by status quo, were philosophically against integrating disabled children into regular educational settings. Many simply didn't want disabled children inside a regular school. In no small measure, this philosophy placed an actual burden on disabled children to earn their seats in the regular classroom, basically by demonstrating that they weren't disabled! In many school districts, the label pinned on a child determined his or her placement in the public school system.

Dual Placement

Mark had just turned three years old. We found a regular preschool program for him to attend in the afternoons with age-appropriate peers. However, concerned over his loss of speech and following guidance from Child Developmental Resources (CDR), we also sought out a special education program for Mark. The school hosting the program was located in Hampton, about twenty-four miles south of our home in Williamsburg. Basically, the program was created for children with communication disorders to help them develop communication skills and augmentative communication systems.

There were five children in Mark's special education class. Mark was the youngest. The other children ranged in age between five and seven years old. Overall, there were twenty students total in the program. The oldest was sixteen years old.

Roxana was probably the first parent ever to volunteer in the special education classroom. Roxana worked at the school two days a week as an aide in the classroom with the older children. Once there, she saw both the good and bad aspects of special education. The first two weeks were the hardest for her. She cried every time she dropped Mark off in the morning, and there were times that Mark would cry too. She tried walking him all the way to the classroom to make it easier on both of them, but it was still hard.

The children in the program were isolated from age-appropriate peers, and this was a definite shortcoming. We were convinced that children with disabilities needed as much contact as possible with their non-disabled peers to learn appropriate behaviors and social skills from them. If placed around other challenged children displaying inappropriate behaviors, a child with disabilities learns inappropriate behavior; placed in integrated settings with non-disabled children displaying more appropriate behaviors, a child with disabilities has increased opportunity to learn *those* behaviors. Nonetheless, we tried not to think about these things, focusing on the fact that Mark had half-days at the afternoon preschool program where he was surrounded by non-disabled peers (indeed, overwhelmed by them!).

Eventually, Roxana volunteered in Mark's classroom. This firsthand look accelerated some of Roxana's concerns about the suitability of special education programs for our son. One bewildering aspect of the program was its approach to handling unwanted behaviors, such as tantrums. After a behavior escalated to an unacceptable level, the child would be carefully wrapped in a sheet to restrict hand, arm, and leg movements, and then taken to a private area to have a time-out period to settle down. The child would be told to stop the behavior in order to be freed from the sheet. Roxana couldn't understand this whole approach; it was so new and different to her. In one instance, the child seemed to spend more time alone and wrapped up in a sheet than in the classroom!

All Roxana could think about was Mark. She thought *What if this should happen to Mark? Would they do this to Mark?* Then Roxana remembered that we had signed a form that authorized program personnel to use any method deemed necessary to control disruptive behaviors. At that time, there was no such thing as "positive behavioral supports," much less "social stories."

We were also disturbed that the program director wouldn't allow Roxana to take pictures or videotape Mark at school. She told Roxana that this decision respected the privacy of the other children in Mark's classroom and preserved their right to confidentiality. Even so, when even simple things like taking Mark's picture became an issue, we were left feeling like we were on an obstacle course. This was the beginning of our own education about public school policies and prerogatives.

In spite of these issues, we kept Mark in the program because we judged that he was learning and that the staff cared for him. This environment also provided us with a safe feeling, as parents. Eventually, we both reached a comfort level with the school's special education practices and felt at ease.

Communication was good between the classroom teacher and home. We used a daily journal to write notes back and forth. Small goals were met rather easily. Big goals came slowly and one at a time. Regardless, it felt good to see Mark making progress at school, coupled with his learning and development at home.

At Home

Puzzles became Mark's favorite thing! We had stacks of puzzles all around the house so that Mark could readily work on a puzzle at will. He had a remarkably long attention span for puzzles, an interest we hoped he might transfer to other areas. Mark also liked to watch cartoons on the television. Nonetheless, we set a limit on the amount of television he could watch and used television time as a motivator or reward for Mark when taking on difficult tasks.

Mark had sleeping problems off and on during those early years. It was truly surprising to us, because our daily routine had worked so well with Laura. Nonetheless, we noticed that Mark would take short cat naps every chance he had, but not get restful sleep until we put him to bed at 8:00 p.m. He usually fell asleep within twenty minutes, but by 11:30 p.m., was fully awake and full of energy. Since Joseph had to work the next day, Roxana would stay up with Mark in his room for hours at a time. It was very draining. It was also a struggle to get him ready for school in the morning and on the bus by 8:20 a.m. After months of these long days and short nights, we requested that the school no longer permit Mark to nap during the school day or on bus rides. Thankfully, in a week or so, Mark's irregular sleep pattern was broken and he was back to sleeping through the night.

Potty training was also a big victory! We implemented a two-week program at school and at home. At school, Mark would be taken into a private area without pants on, just a shirt, where he was given salty snacks to eat and a lot to drink. He learned to sense when he needed to go to the potty and used pictures to let us know. We followed the same program at home, after school and on weekends. We split the duty and took turns. Basically, Roxana would be in charge in the morning and Joseph took over in the afternoon, allowing us at least some time each day to spend with Laura. We rewarded Mark with cold pickles for all his good work! It became a game with him and Mark was a fast learner. In the short span of two weeks, Mark was ready to be totally out of diapers—another blessing!

At home, we set up one of our bedrooms as a playroom. Roxana used structured, one-on-one time to work with Mark on improving his visual, fine motor, and communication skills. We set a schedule for Mark's day and used a picture board to enable him to make choices along the way. From the beginning, we also taught Laura and Mark to pick up their toys after play and to put everything away. A spin off from this was that Mark was always good about not touching household knick-knacks; he acquired a good grasp on boundaries at home. We were encouraged that Mark was responding to rules and limits. These early experiences taught us that Mark was comfortable with structure and with a well-designed routine at home and at school.

Integrated Preschool

As an integral part of his early intervention strategies, we sought an afternoon preschool program where Mark would have opportunities for valuable interaction with non-disabled peers. Finding a program to accept him became a challenge, however. Every place we went, we were turned away the minute the word "autism" was mentioned. Finally and to our relief, one of the preschools accepted Mark. Mark attended this preschool program for a year and a half.

During the first eight months or so, Roxana was Mark's teacher's aide—in fact, this preschool had a lot of parental involvement. As a parent cooperative, all parents were required to serve as a preschool teacher's aide for a set number of hours each year as a condition of their child's enrollment. Our classroom had one teacher and two parents with the children each afternoon. The parents were curious about Mark because he looked so normal; it was hard to notice anything different about him—that is, until he started acting out, due to frustration.

It was so interesting to see how children were totally innocent of Mark, fully accepting him into their play activities, never seeing him as different or strange. Of course, they still made innocent observations. When some children asked, "Why doesn't he talk?" Roxana would answer, "Because God made him that way, just the same way He made little Tommy with black hair and Amanda with blue eyes. We all are different in many ways, and it's those differences that we should accept in other people." She would try to explain it like that. This normally satisfied their curiosity.

The playgroup parents had so many more questions. We became defensive at times, having to justify our son to them. Some of the questions hit straight through to our emotional core, especially when asked about Mark's prognosis. How could we ever predict what the future would hold? How could anyone forecast life for his or her typical child, much less one with autism? But the good news was that we had Mark in a regular school environment in the afternoon with other children. That was good news, for now.

The second year at that preschool turned out to be wonderful. We were so lucky! One of the preschool teachers who normally taught class in the morning volunteered to be Mark's teacher's aide in the afternoon. We were surprised that someone actually wanted to work with Mark ... and for nothing in return! For the first time since our family arrived in Williamsburg, we felt some relief. We will always be grateful for the understanding and love that this wonderful woman had when working with Mark.

Special Therapies

Overall, we were comfortable with Mark's placement in the two different preschool programs. Nonetheless, as we learned more about occupational therapy with sensory integration (OT/SI), we realized that Mark should be receiving therapy. Since the special education program did not provide OT/SI for Mark, we sought an independent evaluation and presented it to our local school district as a recommendation we wanted to pursue. Once the district approved our request, Mark began receiving an hour of private OT/SI therapy four times each week, following his afternoon preschool program. On those days, Roxana would pick Laura up from school and then join Mark and his occupational therapist (OT).

Mark's OT was truly knowledgeable about children with autism. She enjoyed working with Mark and developed a wonderful relationship with him. She knew how far to push him and was sensitive to his frustrations and anxiety. Mark responded well to her. The OT always came loaded with stuff to use while working on Mark's program for the day. In addition to sharing a wealth of great strategies and ideas, the OT projected an upbeat motto, "There's no problem that does not have a solution." We really enjoyed those days! We did tons of brushing, deep pressure massage, and activities to increase Mark's tolerance of textures.

In the process, Roxana learned a lot about OT in general and was, therefore, able to provide Mark with much-needed sensory breaks at home. During those days, Mark would become antsy at home, sometimes to the point of being hyperactive. When appropriate, we spent hours at a time supervising Mark while he enjoyed hot baths with lots of bubbles. Sometimes the shower would be going at the same time! While it sounds kind of crazy, this helped Mark tremendously to relax.

Parents Helping Parents

Through the special education program, we both became active participants in a local parents' support group. Unfortunately, of the twenty families with children in the program, there were only five parents who regularly showed for the monthly support group meetings. It was through this group that we met Cindy Hamrick, another parent whose friendship we have treasured through the years. Cindy's son, Dave, was also enrolled in the special education program in Hampton. He was five years older than Mark and rode the "special ed" bus with Mark to school. Cindy and Roxana would drive together to the monthly support group meetings and, in the end, they became their own two-person mini-support group.

Even though our families have had many similar experiences, Dave and Mark are totally different individuals requiring attention for disparate issues. In a way, the only thing that they have in common is the label, "autism."

Since Dave was older than Mark, Cindy was often in the lead when dealing with new issues. Roxana didn't want to have to reinvent the wheel each time another challenge arose, so she would often try Cindy's strategies to help solve problems with Mark. She was eager to receive Cindy's counsel. Roxana and Cindy would talk regularly, constantly passing on new information and sharing their experiences. They shared books, went to conferences together, and relied upon each other to scan newspapers/newsletters for current information. Prior to the Internet, with information otherwise slow to circulate, this naturally developing support network between our families was invaluable. The two moms laughed and cried a lot together! As we look back on those days, it's interesting to see how much Cindy and Roxana both grew from dealing with the issues that impacted Dave and Mark.

Success with Early Interventions

Some of the efforts we started prior to preschool paid off. Throughout those early years and until Mark reached his fifth birthday, we witnessed a significant decrease in Mark's anxiety level, likely due to his diet. We both became health food junkies and, initially, hoped to discover that magic combination of foods and vitamins that would cure Mark of autism. Without some kind of reward, Mark would refuse to eat the assortment of fruits and vegetables that we prepared especially for him (if left to his own devices, we're sure that he would have eaten nothing else but dry cereal!). While we eventually gave up on finding the magic cure, we still kept our eyes open for anything that could lessen the effects of Mark's autism and were pleased to note his reduced anxiety level, over time.

Communication remained a major issue for Mark. The special education staff at school developed a picture exchange communication system for Mark, paired with sign language. We also used this system at home, changing the pictures according to the setting. Mark was very receptive to pictures and learned how to use them rather quickly. On the other hand, he was not too interested in sign language. Nonetheless, Mark learned to use several helpful signed words.

From the time he could walk, Mark loved the water and became a strong swimmer. Laura and Mark would spend hours at the pool during the summer. Their brother-sister friendship appeared to solidify during this time because they had found something they could do together. Since this was such an enjoyable and bonding experience for them both, we always made sure the children had access to a pool, even during the winter months.

In fact, we regularly planned special activities for both Laura and Mark to enjoy. We often ventured into the community as a family to see a movie, to go to the mall, to a restaurant, or to the library. All of these outings were driven by our desire to make family life with Mark as uncomplicated and as normal as possible. In sum, we wanted to be a supportive, cohesive family. Most importantly, we didn't want to pay so much attention to Mark that we overshadowed Laura's own needs and experiences.

Move to Illinois

So, we continued this established regimen for Mark until our family departed Williamsburg, Virginia, in July 1990. Joseph changed jobs and we moved to Lombard, Illinois. Here in a suburb of Chicago and close to where Joseph grew up, we would be close to his family and on familiar ground.

Before moving, Roxana made a concerted effort to identify educational options for Mark in the Chicago area. Her goal was to line up a dual placement for Mark similar to what he'd had in Williamsburg, incorporating both regular-education and special-education opportunities. In spite of her efforts, we were largely unsuccessful. Now five years old, Mark was simply too old for any preschool program, and we judged that he was not yet ready for the rigors of kindergarten.

At this crossroads, wondering whether Mark would attend kindergarten with his peers, we felt haunted by the special education teacher who had earlier predicted that "a child like Mark may never be able to be in a regular classroom." We couldn't help wonder if that teacher was right!

CHAPTER 4

AN AWAKENING
1991

Shortly after arriving in Lombard, Illinois, we decided to enroll Mark in Keaton Academy (part of Lilly Francis, Inc.) in Naperville, Illinois, about fifteen miles away. Lilly Francis, Inc. offered comprehensive programs that served children with widely varying disabilities throughout the Chicago area. It also offered counseling and guidance to "families in crisis." Keaton Academy specifically focused on children with autism and offered a program to help them meet specified educational goals within a school setting. In general, Lilly Francis had a good reputation in the special education community, and Keaton Academy was widely considered *the center* for autism in the area. Keaton Academy was praised as the school that brought together the right expertise and the best learning strategies to maximize the educational benefit for children with autism.

To enroll Mark at Keaton Academy, we met with the director of Special Education for District 44 Schools, who endorsed the idea and provided the funding for it. Nonetheless, we were mildly anxious about the large size of Lilly Francis/Keaton Academy and that, again, Mark would be the youngest student enrolled there.

Roxana wanted to volunteer time at Lilly Francis just like she had done in Virginia, but she was turned down. The Director of Children's Services was opposed to the idea of parental volunteers as a matter of policy, so there was nothing more that could be done. We were disappointed because Roxana valued the experiences she gained previously as a parent volunteer, experiences that had given her valuable ideas on how to work with Mark at home.

Within weeks, our family settled into a new routine. Mark was in the autism program at Keaton Academy and Laura was in first grade at Saint Pius X Grade School, a parochial school in Lombard. Now that both children were in school, Roxana became involved with the local autism community in Illinois. We all participated in a support group for families who have children with autism. This group brought guest speakers to discuss a wide range of parental issues and concerns, while the children played. At those monthly meetings, there were organized activities for both the children with autism as well as their siblings to enjoy.

Through the support group, Roxana expanded her contacts with medical and education professionals focused on autism, as well as with parents of children of all ages. In talking with parents whose children had attended Keaton Academy, a composite view began to emerge. Basically, children with autism spent years at Keaton Academy without making any noticeable progress. In addition, the parents of the older children with autism (fifteen years and older) appeared beaten down, with little energy left to continue their efforts to make life tolerable for their children.

After gaining this glimpse of the outcomes likely for students enrolled in the autism program at Keaton Academy, we were seriously concerned. We worried that Mark's isolation from typical children while attending Keaton Academy would negatively affect his cognitive and social skill development. Roxana renewed her search for a regular preschool program for Mark, but was turned down time and time again. We felt almost desperate to find a workable scenario to provide Mark the exposure to regular children that we judged he needed for his overall development!

In addition to its programs for children with disabilities, Lilly Francis operated a fairly large day care center as a way to offer child-care services to its staff members. This was key information! Concerned by Mark's lack of progress in developing receptive language skills, we suggested that Keaton Academy allow Mark some daily time in its day care center around age-appropriate peers. After some negotiation, the staff at Keaton Academy agreed to look into the possibility. Once we gained the consent of the staff-parents of children in the day-care program, Mark was scheduled for one hour at the day care center, three times each week. While pleased, we only wished that the school could have done more.

Within a short time, Roxana joined the local Autism Society of America (ASA) chapter and was elected to serve as a member of the ASA Board of Directors for the state of Illinois. Serving on the state board gave Roxana expanded opportunities to meet parents and become further immersed in the issues that impacted children with autism, including legislative initiatives, educational policies, health care, and the provision of services. Roxana found that the ASA Board of Directors for Illinois spent most of its time working on issues related to education, job-training, and the provision of independent but supportive living arrangements for adults with autism outside the confines of state institutions. We were disappointed that few agenda items concerned younger children with autism, preschool through thirteen years of age.

After just over two months at Keaton Academy, we concluded that Mark was not showing any progress with his communication skills. He simply would not accept new pictures on his communication board. Consequently, we sought out a communication system that would be easier for Mark to use, easier to teach him, and, ultimately, more effective. A multi-level computerized device called "The Communicator" appeared to us to be the perfect answer. This computer-like device offered a communication system with simulated voice output that had proven effective for school children with a full-time teacher's aide. The Communicator was larger than most modern laptop computers, about twice as thick, and very fragile. It was not readily mobile, unless strapped to a table affixed to a wheelchair. It cost just over three thousand dollars.

Mark used the Communicator consistently at home, but at a rudimentary level. His performance at school was no better. Over time, the efforts to teach Mark to use the device faded. Even at home, Mark learned to express his wants easily through elementary sign language and his own actions. Within months, the Communicator found its way onto a closet storage shelf. We learned an important lesson: Be cautious about purchasing augmentative communication systems not yet proven effective for children who are non-verbal!

There was a daily journal exchanged between Keaton Academy teachers and home, all about Mark. We began to notice a pattern in the journal entries about Mark crying for one reason or another, but always while going to the physical education (PE) room. Scheduling time to observe Mark in PE, Roxana noticed that Mark became terribly upset just prior to his PE class and cried bitterly all the way to the PE room. To Roxana, it was much like torture for Mark! Other children in his class were also crying and upset. Instinctively, Roxana knew that something wasn't right about all this, but she felt helpless to do anything about it.

Weeks later, we attended a celebration at Keaton Academy with all of the students in attendance. Mark cried during the entire presentation, along with about half of the other children. The teachers ignored them all. It appeared to us that the staff basically treated all of the students alike. Their methods were uncompromising and their strategies inflexible. Basically, nothing changed from one child to another.

Both of us had serious concerns about this one-size-fits-all approach to handling and teaching children with autism. As parents, we had learned that autism can present differently between individual children and that some flexibility in approach may be required to find the best strategies to meet each child's needs. For example, we knew that Mark was *not* difficult to work with as long as he understood beforehand that the activity had a beginning and an end. Otherwise, any activity would seem like sheer torture for him—not knowing when the activity would end. Thus, we wondered if this sort of accommodation was considered and used at school to help individual children meet their needs.

Before long, the time came for us to meet with Mark's teachers at Keaton Academy to formalize Mark's first Individualized Education Plan (IEP). The staff members working with Mark, the director of Special Education and the principal of the school were all preparing to discuss the goals and objectives of the draft IEP in detail. To help us prepare to formalize the school's IEP recommendations, the staff sent us progress reports on Mark's educational program in advance of the meeting.

In reviewing the reports, we found that some of the staff's comments and judgments were simply unfounded. We saw other remarks as totally inaccurate and felt they were likely written about another child. When these observations were brought to the fore, the staff members apologized and agreed to correct the misinformation in the reports as a pre-condition for us signing Mark's new IEP.

This experience caused an important insight to take root in our view of teachers and therapists. First, not all teachers or therapists are equally professional in the performance of their job. Second, not all have an ability to remain objective and unbiased in writing evaluations on the children with whom they work. After all, they are writing, in essence, about "their own successes" or "their own failures" as a teacher/therapist, every time they prepare a child's evaluation. In this way, we felt that the Keaton Academy reports were just too self-serving and inaccurate in this instance.

Also noteworthy during his early months at Keaton Academy, Mark's behavior at home became increasingly more challenging. He cried and used unwanted behaviors with more and more regularity. Moreover, these behaviors were intensifying and becoming potentially harmful. On some occasions, Mark would strike himself on the side of the head, using the back of his hand, to communicate extreme frustration. At the time, we accepted these behaviors as being representative of autism. Nonetheless, we also judged that the escalation in behaviors was directly proportional to Mark's level of frustration at school. For reasons unknown, it became clear that he was not comfortable there. Alternately, once Mark settled into his play routine at home, we saw him much more relaxed and content.

During this same timeframe, Roxana became aware of a new movement called PIC or "Parents for Inclusive Communities," made up of parents and professionals working with children with disabilities of all ages. We both considered the ideas about inclusive communities truly noble. Notwithstanding, and however hopeful, we simply could not picture Mark actually going to his neighborhood school with typical peers. PIC parents spoke with Roxana about children who were being included in grade schools all around the United States, but these children were notably different than Mark. They all could communicate verbally and demonstrate independent cognitive processing abilities. As it were, these were Mark's two most serious developmental deficits, along with limitations in social awareness.

Then we had an awakening that transformed our thinking! During the summer of 1991, we attended ASA's national conference. Cindy Hamrick and her son, Dave, came by train from Williamsburg to Chicago; they then accompanied us to Indianapolis, Indiana, for the week-long conference.

During the conference, we attended lectures given by Ann Donnellan, Ph.D., from the University of Wisconsin. Dr. Donnellan gave a cohesive presentation focused on the importance of an inclusive education for children diagnosed with autism. Her logic was impeccable, and the substance of her seminar was impressive. Dr. Donnellan's research clearly demonstrated that fully included children with autism achieved far better outcomes than those in segregated special education programs. As evidence, she cited the state of Vermont's experience with inclusive education. According to Dr. Donnellan, over 80 percent of children with disabilities in Vermont actually graduate from high school with their typical peers. Furthermore, Vermont had wonderful success placing its disabled population into community-based homes and jobs, thereby drastically reducing the state's reliance on institutional care for its disabled.

Inspired, we returned to Chicago convinced that if we were *ever* going to move Mark to the least restrictive school environment, this was the moment!

CHAPTER 5

INCLUSION - KINDERGARTEN
1991-92

It didn't take long for us to gather more information on "inclusion" and to begin making plans. While Mark attended Keaton Academy for summer school, Roxana requested that the staff there help develop a transition plan to assist Mark in adjusting to kindergarten. Basically, we envisioned a "dual placement" for Mark, with mornings in the special education program at Keaton Academy and afternoons in the regular kindergarten class at Butterfield School, our neighborhood school located just over two blocks from our home.

To help plan Mark's move into a regular kindergarten classroom, Roxana consulted with parents of older children with autism to learn more about their experiences. They all agreed that it would be increasingly more difficult to begin a school inclusion process at an older age. They also said that if they had to do it all over again, that's what they would have done for their own children … included them at school at the first opportunity. These parents cautioned Roxana that we would suffer an emotional toll from dealing with the school system and encouraged us to be strong in facing what would lie ahead. We had heard of several due process fights with school districts over placement issues and the provision of services for children. "Due process," we learned, was the basic legal framework that parents were required to work within to ensure that local school administrators respected their rights under federal law and the rights of children to a free and appropriate education. Although we had heard stories about due process, in reality, we had little appreciation for the devastating impact it has on children, parents, and entire families.

Moving forward with our plan for dual placement, together we stopped by the District 44 school offices to speak with the director of Pupil Services. After we explained our proposal for Mark's dual placement, the director candidly commented that placing Mark in a regular kindergarten was not recommended and suggested that we keep him enrolled, full time, at Keaton Academy. Nonetheless, the director agreed to explore kindergarten for Mark at the neighborhood school and said that we should first meet with the principal of Butterfield School, Ms. Sandra "Sandy" K. Truax. Within days, he arranged the meeting, which would also include several staff members from the District 44 central office. Beyond that, we didn't know what to expect.

The meeting with Ms. Truax was cordial, informative and goal oriented. She was precise in her comments and expressed a strong interest in Mark. During the meeting, Ms. Truax said that she wanted to meet Mark and to observe him at Keaton Academy. The first request was easily accomplished. Roxana and Mark stopped by Butterfield School to introduce him to Ms. Truax and to acquaint him with the school building. Then, Roxana coordinated with Keaton Academy for Ms. Truax to observe Mark in class. Ms. Truax invited select kindergarten teachers and staff members to go with her.

Things looked positive after that first visit. Ms. Truax asked Roxana to arrange another meeting with the Keaton Academy staff to begin planning for Mark's transition into kindergarten. During this meeting, details were fleshed out concerning necessary preparations for Butterfield School. This included plans for staff training in autism, positive behavior support strategies, and augmentative communication, as well as planning for occupational therapy and transportation. Ms. Truax contacted a child psychologist in Chicago with an established expertise in autism; she relied upon this psychologist to engage the staff and help them better understand autism. She also worked with specialists from the district's special education program to enhance the Butterfield School staff's understanding of inclusion and to create a team mentality. Ms. Truax told us that she would also hire a paraprofessional to assist Mark in the classroom as an instructional aide, and that they would rely upon the direction and guidance of an inclusion coordinator to organize and implement Mark's program correctly. Ms. Truax explained that the inclusion coordinator, an experienced special education teacher with regular education experience as well, worked out of the District 44 central office and would serve as the coordinator for inclusion at Butterfield School. Finally, Ms. Truax told Roxana that she saw no need to plan for intrusion therapy, since Mark would have twenty or so "intruders" in the classroom with him on a daily basis. Her comment gave a glimpse into the wonderful sense of humor embodied in this consummate professional!

Interestingly and unbeknownst to us, District 44 was exploring the issue of inclusion, trying to determine the training requirements and resource allocation that would be necessary to make it a success. An inclusion coordinator was already working on the district's staff and was supervising the partial inclusion of a handful of children from special education in the regular school classroom. Nonetheless, *Mark would be the first child with autism to be fully included by District 44!* Butterfield School would be their test bed to gauge whether or not inclusion was advisable across the board for other children with disabilities.

Once the ball got rolling, we realized there was no turning back. Ms. Truax had taken the lead and was putting all of the pieces together. She coordinated directly with the staff at Keaton Academy to ensure that her teachers were sufficiently prepared to have Mark in their classroom. Strategies were discussed and scheduling options were reviewed. Additionally, Ms. Truax encouraged the occupational and speech therapists to become involved in the preparations. It was obvious that Ms. Truax had taken ownership of Mark's inclusion program and was doing everything prudent to ensure a smooth-running program and successful outcome. Her positive approach and ardent determination were reflected throughout the entire staff at Butterfield School, as we all faced this challenge together.

By coincidence, Joseph knew the inclusion coordinator working to prepare the Butterfield School staff for Mark's inclusion in kindergarten. Joanne Bade and Joseph attended the same high school. Her husband and Joseph's older brother, George, were in the same class and remained friends through the years. Most importantly, we felt total trust in Ms. Bade, knowing that she would be candid in discussing Mark's program and fully committed.

Periodically, Ms. Truax called Roxana to update her on planning. They had one final meeting to review the details of Mark's kindergarten schedule, breaks and therapy sessions. Mark was to continue the placement at Keaton Academy in the morning, eat lunch there, and then come by bus to Butterfield School in time for the start of afternoon kindergarten. The instructional assistant would meet Mark when he got off the bus and remain with him throughout the kindergarten activities. Everyone anxiously awaited September 1991's start of school and the launch of Mark's dual placement.

Mark adjusted wonderfully to his new routine. He especially liked kindergarten, even the challenge of coping with twenty other children in his class. Roxana visited Butterfield School occasionally to review Mark's status with Ms. Truax and to observe Mark in the classroom.

Having Mark attend Butterfield School gave Roxana the opportunity to become a part of the Parent-Teacher Association (PTA). The parents were very positive about inclusion at the grade school level. Very quickly, Roxana learned that Ms. Truax led by example and was ushering both her staff and the parents into this new age of inclusive education. She had created an environment at Butterfield School that embraced the diversity of all the children. Additionally, Ms. Truax ensured that teacher morale was high and that all issues were fairly resolved. Moreover, she made sure that we always felt welcomed at school.

We considered Mark's experiences at Butterfield School to be a wonderful success for everyone! By late winter, we asked to see Ms. Truax to discuss preparations for Mark's first grade year. We knew that the decision to allow Mark to advance to first grade would be an IEP decision. Nevertheless, we wanted the reassurance of knowing what Ms. Truax had in mind to ensure proper planning. Her answer was simple: As far as she was concerned, Mark would move to first grade with his class! He had demonstrated steady improvement and progress throughout kindergarten. Ms. Truax said that she was already working on plans for the transition and staff training. We were at the threshold of a new educational experience for Mark! Anticipating Mark's inclusion at Butterfield School's full day, fully integrated first grade in the fall, his attendance at Keaton Academy ended in May 1992.

CHAPTER 6

INCLUSION – FIRST GRADE
1992-93

When school began in September 1992, Butterfield School was ready for Mark's entry into first grade. The students in Mark's class were pretty much the same children from kindergarten, with only six or seven new additions. Ms. Truax purposely planned for Mark to be with children already familiar with him, to make his transition to first grade as easy as possible. He would be among friends, but with a new one-on-one aide and teacher.

Over the summer, Roxana had taken Mark to visit Butterfield School several times to reacquaint him with the classroom environment and to prepare him for first grade. During each visit, Mark was receptive and comfortable with school. It was convenient that the school was just a few blocks down the street from our home. After the first few weeks, Mark began to ride his bike to school, like many other children in the neighborhood. Of course, his blue bicycle still had training wheels, and one of us had to accompany him on foot to ensure his safety—but we were so pleased to have Mark going off to school just like any other first grader!

Ms. Truax interviewed applicants for the instructional aide position and selected Ms. Mary Ann Mrazek, an experienced primary school teacher who had worked part time at Butterfield School and wanted to get back into the classroom. Both Ms. Mrazek and the first grade teacher worked with Mark's kindergarten teacher and with Ms. Bade, the inclusion coordinator, in preparation for Mark's arrival to first grade.

In addition to curriculum adaptations provided by Ms. Bade, Ms. Mrazek used her experience and imagination to make on-the-spot modifications to Mark's curriculum, when required. Most importantly, Ms. Mrazek developed a relationship with Mark that was something special. She always spoke with Mark in a soft and understanding tone of voice that calmed him. Ms. Mrazek was also patient with Mark and seemed to know instinctively when he needed a break from the classroom routine.

Since first grade was a full day program, the IEP team agreed that Mark could go home during the forty-five minute lunch period for a long sensory break. Following lunch, Roxana would give Mark a hot bubble bath, which he loved. The hot, relaxing bath, mid-day, also helped prepare him for two more hours of school each afternoon. We knew that by making the hot bath part of Mark's routine and part of the structure of his day, the rigors of a first grade classroom would be easier for Mark to tolerate. Our strategy proved successful—Mark's unwanted behaviors diminished significantly, as did his frustration level.

To address Mark's anxiety over physical education (PE), Ms. Truax arranged for an adaptive PE instructor to consult with the school. An individualized approach to teaching PE was key, as Mark needed one that accommodated him during drills and let him have the freedom to enjoy himself. Accordingly, the PE teacher always took time at the beginning of the class to give Mark one-on-one attention; then, on his own, Mark required little assistance as he mimicked his classmates. Within weeks, Mark began to show a new comfort level with PE never seen before. In time, he even appeared to love every moment of it!

Over all, Mark was comfortable in his first-grade class. OT and speech therapy continued on a regular schedule, and Mark enjoyed both. In kindergarten, Mark had learned to tolerate having his classmates close to him and how to take turns during group activities. These experiences transferred well to first grade. PE continued without incident, and Mark's receptive language continued to improve. He understood the daily class routine and was eager to move from one period to another throughout the day. Mark even participated in the Christmas pageant with his class. Classmates sang while Mark played the tambourine to the beat of a Christmas song. Everyone at school marveled at Mark's accomplishments! We randomly took videotapes of Mark at school to create a record of his progress.

Mark's crying bouts, experienced almost daily at Keaton Academy, were now rare. Mark's vocal sounds continued, but everyone at school understood that these sounds were part of his communication and not just part of his behavior. Ms. Mrazek was especially adept at interpreting the specific meanings behind Mark's vocal sounds, understanding that his vocalizations conveyed things such as: *I'm content and enjoying myself; This is fun; This is bothersome for me;* or *I can't stand this—please give me a break!* Her instincts and interpretive ability allowed her to serve as a role model for other students/teachers and gave Mark the reassurance that he would never be forced into anything that he couldn't tolerate. So "heard," Mark grew comfortable and confident with Ms. Mrazek at school. To further expand opportunities for his communication in class, Mark also used pictures on a communication board and a picture schedule for transitions.

During this same time, Facilitated Communication (FC) was gaining momentum throughout the United States as a viable method for children with autism to communicate their thoughts and desires. FC incorporates the touch of a trusted person on the hand/arm/shoulder of the person wanting to type out words and thoughts. The level of support (or touch) required depends upon how practiced the individual with autism is in using FC, as well as his/her confidence in the facilitator. While there's a lot going on when Mark facilitates, if the facilitator has confidence in what s/he is doing, there is no problem ... Mark will be able to communicate via FC, regardless of whether he knows the facilitator personally or not. On the other hand, if the facilitator is not confident and experienced with this technique, Mark will sense it and his facilitated communication will be strained, if successful at all. We saw FC as a means to an end—a way to help Mark achieve free-flowing communication. As such, we pursued FC at the rudimentary level to introduce Mark to the power of words. At home, we made flash cards and labeled all of the items in the kitchen so Mark could see and understand that everything had a name. We also arranged for Mark to receive more time with his speech therapist. Finally, through Ms. Truax and Ms. Bade, we made sure that everyone at school working with Mark received basic training in facilitated communication.

Positive Results

All these positive efforts seemed to pay off as Mark experienced further success as a fully included first-grader. The speech and language pathologist assigned to Mark closed her February 1993 evaluation with the following comments:

> Mark's behavior is not always on target, but he is not disruptive to our school. It is wonderful to see how he has modeled his classmates' behavior. His eye contact is actually quite good. Mark smiles often and it is evident he enjoys school and his relationships. He displays a delightful sense of humor. While Mark has his "lazy, falling out" days, they have been the exception rather than the rule.

While the school staff appeared to enjoy working with Mark, the first grade teacher initially harbored doubts about him and the practice of "inclusion." In a teacher's report dated January 29, 1993, the teacher wrote:

Mark has been an inclusion student at Butterfield School for the last year and a half. In kindergarten, he was assigned to the class across the hall from mine for its half-day session and also attended a half-day program in the morning for autistic children. All year I could hear him and I heard stories of his behavior, some of which I saw for myself. At that time, he could only work on things for very brief periods of time and he could not stay seated. He was very physical when trying to express his dislike for something. Therefore, when it appeared that Mark would be assigned to a first grade classroom full time, I became very concerned and even wrote a letter to the superintendent. I just didn't think a child with autistic behaviors could adjust and benefit from a regular education classroom.

How wrong I was. Mark was assigned to my classroom of nineteen children and he has made much progress this year. I attribute this to our dedicated staff and to the very positive role models he has in this full-time program. He now sits quietly for much of his work and many times it is hard to tell him from other children. He rarely has the tantrums I had seen in kindergarten and we can quickly get a reversal with a "Quiet, Mark" or similar command.

A very qualified instruction assistant is assigned to Mark and I could not do my job as a classroom teacher without her.

My school district has been very good about sending all of us working with Mark to various programs on facilitated communication and autism. None of us had dealt with autistic children before. These programs really helped us to understand the problems Mark has and taught us strategies to deal with them in a professional way.

We have seen much growth in Mark since he started in the fall. He now feels very comfortable in large groups of children and he doesn't mind sitting in the midst of them for calendar or story time or for an all-school assembly. He usually appears very interested and doesn't use self-stimulating noises. The other children in my class have been great with him and praise Mark constantly when he gives a right answer if I call on him. They ignore his inappropriate behavior on a bad day and they are able to continue their work without any problem. I would say that Mark's presence has been a very positive influence on his classmates. They have shown much compassion for him and try to help whenever possible. Because of their excellent modeling, I feel that Mark's behavior has improved this year.

We were overjoyed, things were going well! In a letter dated February 12, 1993, Ms. Truax wrote the following report concerning Mark and his inclusion at Butterfield School:

> (With support) Mark is fully included in the first-grade program. He is a participating member of a reading group supported by his instructional assistant. Mark maintains the same schedule as his classmates.
>
> This opportunity has been extremely successful for all involved, primarily Mark. This year we have noted dramatic, positive changes for this young man. He demonstrates willingness to parallel his peers and occasionally engage in activities, particularly on the playground and computer instruction. We have also noted great strides in appropriate first-grade behavior. Mark has shown tremendous improvement in maintaining eye contact with his peers and adults.... Throughout this effort we have maintained close team communication. The school has also been supported in a most positive way by Mark's parents.

Mark's abilities were also confirmed by several evaluative tests administered at Butterfield School. While the Stanford-Binet Intelligence Scale sub-tests and the Peabody Picture Vocabulary test were unsuccessful because Mark was not cooperative during testing, other evaluations were completed with positive result. The sub-test of the Kaufman Assessment Battery for Children resulted in a score of 110, which placed Mark at the seventy-fifth percentile of the standardization sample. This score indicated that Mark was within the average range. Mark achieved similar results with the Wechsler Preschool Test and the Primary Scale of Intelligence Test. Mark achieved a scaled score of nine, again scoring within the average ability range.

Job Transfer to Virginia

Given such success at Butterfield School, it was with great regret that we learned, in January 1993, that our family would need to relocate to Northern Virginia due to Joseph's job transfer. Even though neither of us looked forward the move, we both knew that there was no choice. Realizing how much work and preparation it took to have Mark fully included at Butterfield School, Roxana started preparations *early* to ensure an easy and smooth transition for Mark into second grade, in Virginia.

So we would have a comparative view for the record, Roxana invited the staff from Keaton Academy to observe Mark in first grade. She requested a written report of their observations. Mark's preschool teacher at Keaton Academy, Ms. Michelle Meyers, visited Butterfield School to observe Mark during his morning classes. She had participated in the training/discussions for the Butterfield School staff prior to kindergarten, was curious about the progress that Mark had made, and looked upon the invitation as an opportunity to learn something about inclusion. The following excerpts are from Ms. Meyers' report:

> In this fully inclusive setting, Mark was very capable of following the classroom routine utilizing his photo/written word schedule independently. He was aware of set classroom routines such as the "morning opening" and could participate with little assistance from his personal aide. Mark was able to write number concepts on the blackboard with light physical assistance.
>
> During reading group, Mark participated fully with his first grade peers. He independently found the correct page in his reading book and was able to answer questions by pointing to words in the book or using his Canon Communicator and facilitated communication. The Canon Communicator is a compact battery-powered keyboard that prints what is typed on a paper tape. Mark was able to do reading comprehension questions by pointing to the correct pictures on a worksheet or by typing single word answers on his Canon. Often, if the worksheet involved copying the word, Mark used his Canon with no facilitation from his personal aide. It should be noted that Mark's classroom staff did not typically have to use different materials with Mark, but rather adapted the regular first grade materials to provide Mark with a way to respond.
>
> During this observation, Mark was scheduled to go to speech therapy; however, once he got there, he found that the speech therapist wasn't in that day. Mark was able to handle this change in schedule well.... When Mark was at Keaton Academy, changes in schedule were much more difficult for him than currently.
>
> ...Mark followed along well with math and color activities such as coloring correct spaces based on the number correspondence in the spaces. Mark also was able to do simple addition problems independently by circling the correct response. He became a bit agitated and restless in a capitalization and punctuation activity that may not have been as meaningful or motivating for Mark.

…Generally, Mark was able to sit at his desk for longer periods of time than when he was at Keaton Academy. He also seemed less bothered by noise distractions such as the pencil sharpener. He waited patiently for his turn in an activity as well as in line.

…Gym class was more difficult for Mark, although he attempted to participate fully. In this activity the "rules" were very flexible, the space large, and children moving in all different directions which may have made it more difficult for Mark to understand his "role" in this setting. However, he was able to participate and attempted to imitate his first grade peers' actions well.

In summary, Mark appears to have made a nice growth in his academic skills in this fully inclusive setting. He has also demonstrated increased independence, and continues to improve in his communication skills through the use of facilitated communication and other augmentative systems. Although some adaptations had to be implemented to allow Mark to respond to first grade activities, in general, he seemed to be following the curriculum well.

It is a pleasure to observe a former student being so successful. It is hoped that all future school placements will look at what has been done with Mark over the past three years in all his settings to contribute to the success he has today and to continue that growth in the future.

For us, this report evidenced not only Mark's measurable progress over the past year, but also the success of Ms. Truax's commitment and dedication to his full inclusion at Butterfield School. We certainly saw how much Mark benefitted from those efforts, but it was heartwarming to see professionals from two separate schools, both current and former, also recognize the progress Mark made following his full inclusion with peers. These results seemed conclusive, yet the unknown awaited us in Virginia.

CHAPTER 7

NORTHERN VIRGINIA
1993

In late February 1993, when Roxana walked into the offices of Fairfax County Public Schools, she sensed an air of intellectual arrogance that she had never before encountered in dealing with educational professionals. After introducing herself to one of the special education program directors, Roxana said, "My son, Mark, is currently in first grade in Butterfield School in Lombard, Illinois. He is a fully included child with autism with a severe developmental delay in speech. We are moving to Northern Virginia in the summer and plan to settle in Fairfax County. I'm here to begin the process to have Mark fully included in second grade."

Pausing for a moment, the program director then explained that autistic children within Fairfax County were educated in the autism program at the Navy Elementary School located near Franklin Farms subdivision. While some disabled kids were capable enough to be mainstreamed into a class or two, he confirmed that this was certainly *not* the rule. In fact, the special education program director emphasized that Fairfax County just *didn't do* inclusion.

"Maybe I'm not making *myself* clear," Roxana responded. "Mark has been fully included beginning with kindergarten. He's now doing very well in first grade. Mark was the first child with autism to be included in Lombard…and he can be the first in Fairfax County, as well."

Despite admiring Roxana's commitment to her son, the program director clarified that Fairfax County Public Schools (FCPS) could not make any plans for Mark until the Hartmanns actually moved to the county. He added that once Mark became a resident, FCPS would be happy to discuss his educational program, but not before—those were the rules.

We had run into the proverbial catch-22!

We were disappointed and particularly disturbed by the boldness of Fairfax County's set position against inclusion. Further, FCPS showed no concern whatsoever about its apparent disregard for the Individuals with Disabilities Education Act (IDEA), a federal law passed in 1990 that basically guaranteed *an appropriate education in the least restrictive environment for all children with disabilities.*

Weeks later, during a business trip to Washington, D.C., Joseph spoke with the Director of Special Education for Fairfax County over the telephone. Basically, she told Joseph that there was nothing that the school district could do for us at that juncture—that they would certainly not plan to educate Mark before we moved into the county.

Interrupting Joseph as he was trying to make a point, the director asserted that Fairfax County *didn't have* a full inclusion program. Furthermore, she relayed that it was against FCPS policy to assign a one-on-one aide to any special education student—or to decide placement without a complete evaluation beforehand. The kicker? This director of special education added that *it didn't matter* what the IEP from Illinois said! Joseph judged that the director was only tolerating him as he continued to emphasize the legal requirement for Fairfax Schools to implement Mark's IEP as a transferring student. The director then concluded the conversation by saying that if we came to Fairfax County, that more than likely, Mark would be placed into FCPS's autism program at the designated center. She added that the appropriate expertise to deal with his disability resided at *that* program. Without any courtesy, she abruptly hung up, thereby ending the conversation. Joseph was aghast at the arrogance of this *public servant!*

We knew that including Mark in second grade would demand focused attention, considerable staff training, and the expertise of an experienced inclusion specialist. On the surface, it appeared that Fairfax County wasn't positioned to meet that challenge. Its heavy-handed attitude in dealing with parents was also a non-starter.

Although shocking, our encounter with Fairfax County Public Schools was not entirely unexpected. We wanted to start the process of enrolling Laura and Mark in school in Northern Virginia as early as possible to ensure a smooth transition. As such, Roxana had made several telephone calls to the Northern Virginia Chapter of the Autism Society of America (ASA) to talk with other parents about schools, educational philosophies, and special education. She found out that including Mark in regular second grade in Northern Virginia presented major obstacles to overcome. From her conversations with ASA chapter members, Roxana was left with the impression that, while Fairfax County had a reputation for educational excellence, its excellence focused on programs for gifted and talented students that numbered less than ten percent of their enrollment. Programs for children with disabilities were offered at "centers" located in designated schools throughout the county. These programs were based on labels: MR Program for the Mental Retardation; SMR Program for the Severely Mentally Retarded; Autism Program; ED Program for the Emotionally Disturbed; and so on. According to the well-informed parents in Northern Virginia, Fairfax County Schools did not include any children with disabilities in the regular classroom. Nonetheless, Roxana learned that mainstreaming was possible for select students whom had "proven that they could handle it."

Loudoun County Public Schools

After hearing Fairfax County's stonewalling position, we decided to seek other alternatives in Virginia for Mark's education. Loudoun County Public Schools (LCPS) surfaced as a good option.

Roxana contacted the office of Ms. Meagan Kelly, Director of Special Education in Loudoun County, with an informal enquiry. Roxana remembers that the response was cooperative and understanding. Ms. Kelly assured Roxana that LCPS would honor and implement Mark's IEP as designed and approved by the educational team at Butterfield School. Their only requirement was that we would have to reside in Loudoun County. The location of our house would dictate which neighborhood grade school Mark would attend. LCPS advised that planning for Mark's inclusion in second grade would begin as soon as we had an address in Loudoun County.

On the down side, Roxana learned that LCPS had never fully included any child with autism into the regular classroom, either. Mark would be their first.

On March 23, 1993, we sent Ms. Kelly a letter of formal introduction. We provided her with the most recent written reports from the professionals working with Mark at Butterfield School, as well as video clips of Mark at home and at school. We intended for this material to assist LCPS in its efforts to preplan for Mark's 1993-94 school year and to offer LCPS staff members the opportunity to become acquainted with Mark on paper and via videotape.

We kept in touch with Ms. Kelly and sent a copy of Mark's 1993-94 IEP for second grade, as approved on May 13, 1993 at his annual IEP meeting held at Butterfield School. Joseph also videotaped the IEP meeting, hoping that it would help LCPS staff realize that Mark had been successfully included in first grade—that the accomplishments made at Butterfield School were real, not imagined.

In August 1993, we placed a bid on a new house in Ashburn, Virginia (Loudoun County) and began the process of registering Mark and Laura in school. Shortly thereafter, on August 20, 1993, Ms. Kelly set a meeting at Ashburn Elementary School (Ashburn E.S.), the neighborhood school, to discuss plans for Mark's inclusion program. Ms. Kelly (director of special education in Loudoun County), Ms. Lynn C. Meadows (principal of Ashburn E.S.), Ms. Cristina F. Conroy-Winters (speech and language pathologist), Ms. Debra V. Jarrett (second-grade teacher), and Mr. Erwin Dotson (assistant principal), attended the meeting and, with us, comprised Mark's new IEP team.

The initial meeting with LCPS was cordial. As Director of Special Education, Ms. Kelly presided over the meeting and served as the dominant spokesman for the gathered professionals. The major issue facing the IEP team was the screening and selection of a one-on-one teaching assistant for Mark. LCPS accepted in its entirety Mark's 1993-94 second grade IEP, as approved by Butterfield School. There was no mention of testing Mark with any sort of additional performance evaluations.

The following summary was written on the IEP form that was signed at the end of the meeting by all present: "Mark is currently functioning on a late first-grade level in reading and math. The most recent IEP notes that Mark uses his Canon Communicator and Facilitated Communication (FC) in making choices and answering questions. Mark's strengths are in math, a sense of technology, and in observing. Weaknesses were noted in being able to use FC with everyone as well as handling change. A teaching assistant accompanies Mark in the classroom and in the school environment."

Overall, we were satisfied with our first meeting with LCPS. Both Laura and Mark would attend Ashburn E.S. While everything appeared to be working out just fine, we had no idea that we were entering a period in our lives that would become our worst nightmare in less than one year.

CHAPTER 8

SECOND GRADE
1993-94

In the summer of 1993, Ashburn Elementary School (Ashburn E.S.) was an integral part of a massive contemporary housing development called Ashburn Village, located in one of the fastest growing suburbs of Washington, D.C. Relatively close to Washington's Dulles International Airport and with easy access to a newly-constructed toll road, Ashburn Village was conveniently situated for commuters who worked in downtown Washington.

Ashburn E.S. had a capacity of 800-plus students, kindergarten through fifth grade, including a self-contained preschool for children with disabilities. Having opened in 1991, Ashburn E.S. was considered the showcase of a modern primary school.

September through December 1993

The staff at Ashburn E.S. was caught in a difficult position when school began in September 1993. Even though LCPS had known since March 1993 that we would likely move to Loudoun County, they had not known which specific elementary school would be receiving Mark as a fully included student. As a result, no specific training had been planned for or provided to LCPS personnel pertaining to autism or Mark's inclusion. Furthermore, LCPS provided absolutely no training to its supervisory or administrative personnel. This was of particular concern since LCPS had never before included any child with autism in their regular school program and, in truth, had little idea of what was involved.

At that time, there were several notable resources available to school systems in Virginia, LCPS included. Technical Assistance Center (TAC) offices throughout Virginia routinely offered training and educational services on special education issues, including augmentative communication, assistive technology, accommodation planning, positive behavioral supports, transition planning, and curriculum adaptations for regular classroom curriculums. George Mason University (in Fairfax County) provided a TAC for Northern Virginia school districts, including schools in Loudoun County. These services were available free of charge. In addition, the State of Virginia provided funding for the Virginia Institute of Developmental Disabilities (VIDD) to consult with school districts experiencing difficulties in providing education services to children with disabilities. *Unfortunately for us, LCPS did not use any of these resources to prepare for Mark's arrival at school.* In short, Ashburn E.S. remained markedly unprepared!

Ashburn E.S. principal, Ms. Meadows, interviewed and selected a teaching assistant (TA) to work with Mark. LCPS director of special education Ms. Kelly was on vacation, and therefore, was not consulted on the choice of Mark's TA. Acting on Roxana's suggestion, the TA was introduced to Mark prior to the first day of school, just to get acquainted. Although the TA was a working mother without any specific background or expertise in education, it appeared that she was a good match for Mark. She appeared mellow and laid back in personality, and spoke in a soft voice. We liked these qualities, which would likely form the cornerstone of the personal relationship between Mark and the TA.

Mark had repeatedly demonstrated hypersensitivity to loud music and raised voices, both at home and at school. This became well known at school. To protect himself from such intense sounds, Mark instinctively would press the palms of his hands hard over his ears and make vocal sounds that indicated his hypersensitivity and displeasure with the noise. With the TA's quiet demeanor, we were reassured that the person who would be closest to Mark each day would likely always speak with him softly and in a kind manner. Indeed, as the days turned into weeks, she developed an excellent personal relationship with Mark. He appeared comfortable in and reassured by her presence.

Roxana sought regular contact with the second-grade teacher, Ms. Jarrett, Ashburn's speech/language pathologist, Ms. Conroy-Winters, and with the TA, to offer them her insights in working with Mark. In addition, she gave Ms. Jarrett books to help her develop an understanding and appreciation for autism as a disability. From the start, it seemed to us that the teaching team woefully lacked training in inclusion, lacked personal experience with autism, and was unsure of what was expected of it.

Nevertheless, we were confident that, with training and guidance from Ms. Kelly acting as the inclusion coordinator, Mark's second grade experience would eventually become a positive experience for everyone involved. We knew this would take time and were prepared to be patient. (Note: In spite of the hopefulness of the moment, Ms. Kelly never provided any direct teacher training, nor did she ever modify the teacher's curriculum/lesson plans to accommodate Mark. In addition, she never worked with Mark's teacher's aide to help her understand her role with Mark in the classroom, nor did she prepare positive behavior support or crisis intervention plans for the staff's use with Mark at school.)

We were shocked that the TA received no formal training from LCPS to prepare her for the role of teacher's assistant in Mark's classroom. LCPS appeared to look past the TA—to discount her—only asking that she assist Mark in the classroom, without further defining her role. Except for her attendance at IEP meetings, the TA did not seem to be included in the decision-making process as it affected Mark. Although she was the one working closest and most often with him in the classroom, the TA was often marginalized during discussions of Mark's program. It was common for the teaching staff to continually minimize her point of view; after all, the TA had no credentials or certification in education. The other members of the teaching team failed to recognize that the TA had the closest working relationship with Mark and knew him best.

These circumstances contrasted sharply with our experiences at Butterfield School. There, Ms. Mrazek, Mark's instructional assistant, played a key role on the school's educational team and was active in every aspect of Mark's inclusion program.

Likewise, as far as we could see, LCPS did not offer any substantial training or in-service guidance to Ms. Jarrett on inclusion or autism to prepare her with effective teaching strategies for use with Mark in the second-grade classroom. Nonetheless, facilitated communication (FC) was a component of Mark's IEP. Thus, early in the fall, Ms. Jarrett arranged a primer on FC with Ms. Julie R. Hunt, a speech-language pathologist from the Grafton School in Berryville, Virginia, who was skilled in this communication method. On September 14th, Ms. Hunt came to Ashburn E.S. for a consultation visit. She provided feedback regarding the implementation of FC at school, per Mark's IEP. Spending a little more than three hours at the school, Ms. Hunt worked with Ms. Jarrett to provide her with a basic overview of FC. During her visit, Ms. Hunt also met with Ms. Conroy-Winters, Mark, and Roxana to discuss Mark's use of FC, to observe Mark using FC, and to act as Mark's facilitator herself. Her report was very positive, overall.

From her observations, Ms. Hunt made seven specific recommendations on how the teaching team should use FC as part of Mark's communication plan continuum. In spite of our repeated efforts to encourage follow-through, we never saw consistent implementation of Ms. Hunt's recommendations at any time during second grade at Ashburn E.S. In retrospect, we conclude that the lack of consistency at school concerning FC contributed to Mark's regression in the areas of communication, self-esteem and behavior.

From our perspective, there was no doubt that Ms. Jarrett's lack of experience with inclusion, her unfamiliarity with FC, and her first-time exposure to a child with autism presented a daunting challenge. It would have been the same for any second-grade teacher. By any other measure, she appeared to us to be an excellent teacher, just a total novice concerning inclusion. The methodology required to successfully meet the challenge of full inclusion remained unclear to Ms. Jarrett throughout the school year, in spite of our best efforts to clarify and define it for her.

Additionally, there was no one (i.e., no inclusion facilitator) to assist Ms. Jarrett week-in and week-out with curriculum modifications for Mark, to help solve problems, or to develop effective and appropriate teaching strategies. Educational consultants visited Ms. Jarrett's classroom and wrote their reports. Ms. Kelly and other well-meaning administrators from LCPS central office were involved on a part-time basis and had a lot of advice for Ms. Jarrett. When viewed as a composite, however, the consultants and administrators presented Ms. Jarrett with varying viewpoints on inclusion and on how to teach a child with autism; these differing viewpoints were, at times, diametrically opposed and must have served to confound the teacher.

It was significant that not one of them supported Ms. Jarrett to relieve her of any of the workload required for Mark's inclusion. From our perspective, there was no one, knowledgeable professional working with Ms. Jarrett to ensure that Mark's inclusion program was structured correctly, handled appropriately, and developed to meet the goals on his IEP. This was a far different arrangement in structure and program management than we expected, having just come from Butterfield School!

It was clear to us that the principal at Ashburn E.S., Ms. Meadows, had not received enough training on inclusion, either. Ms. Meadows participated in a two-hour after-school workshop on inclusion in the fall of 1993 and attended a one-day workshop in April 1994, just one month before Mark's second-grade inclusion program came to an end. What a contrast this was to Ms. Truax, principal at Butterfield School, who spearheaded the school's preparation for, overall embrace of, and eventual success with Mark's inclusion.

While Ms. Kelly and Ms. Conroy-Winters were part of a system's change process years before we arrived in Loudoun County, it was unclear if that experience had any positive or measurable impact on them. Except for Ms. Kelly's willingness to at least offer inclusion for Mark, there wasn't any other indication that the system's change process had changed anything in Loudoun County regarding special education. (Note: At that time, Loudoun County had completed all of the prerequisites for system's change, meaning that the school district had completed the required personnel training needed to begin its transformation from strict, segregated placements for children with severe disabilities to inclusive placements, where appropriate.)

Despite the lack of adequate planning and preparation, and even though the going was rough during the first weeks of the school year, we were impressed with the effort that Ms. Jarrett and Ms. Conroy-Winters were making to implement Mark's IEP as approved by Butterfield School. Both of these professionals were enthusiastic and excited with the mini-successes that they were seeing in Mark's performance.

We were pleased that the initial reports from Ashburn E.S. staff were favorable. At the end of the first eight-week grading period, both Ms. Jarrett and Ms. Conroy-Winters wrote up-beat and positive narrative report cards for Mark. Those reports documented many of the same skills evidenced in the final Butterfield School evaluations.

For example, Ms. Jarrett wrote, "I believe he can read quite quickly and often understands what he is reading."

According to her report, "Mark stays on task in reading group for a good 15 minutes daily." Further, "He can put the correct number sticker next to the (math) facts that the TA had written out for him," and "I believe he can spell many consonant-vowel-consonant words independently."

Ms. Conroy-Winters wrote, "Mark is able to point to whole word choices and copy words to answer questions."

She also wrote, "He is also able to point to yes or no accurately."

Additionally, Ms. Conroy-Winters wrote, "When the word that makes the sentence complete is very familiar to Mark, he can work at this level with great consistency."

According to her report, "Mark has typed in approximately seven sentences for me over the course of these nine weeks…. These are spontaneous answers such as 'I want a rest' to the question, 'What do you need, Mark?'" And finally, Ms. Conroy-Winters wrote, "Mark has been a joy to work with."

Nonetheless, toward the beginning of the second quarter grading period, Roxana sensed a change in her relationship with literally all of the members of the teaching team at Ashburn E.S., and even with Ms. Kelly. For lack of anything specific, Roxana described it as "just a perception of a change in attitude" within the group. Progressively, the staff became much less available to her. It also appeared that Ms. Meadows (principal), Mr. Dotson (assistant principal), and others became passive about working with us to address problems and resolve issues concerning Mark's inclusion.

We were both alarmed by the increasing amount of attention being placed on testing and validating Mark's academic abilities, including his use of facilitated communication. To our dismay, this focus continued unabated until the end of second grade. To be clear on this point, there was no systematic, structured program used to teach Mark his daily lessons. Instead, Mark was bombarded with a wide variety of tests on a near-weekly basis to determine his skills in math, reading, and in the use of FC as a communication method. The other children in Mark's classroom were not plagued by anything even remotely close to this testing regimen.

Around this same time, it appeared to us that Ms. Jarrett and Ms. Conroy-Winters began paying less attention to teaching Mark according to his IEP goals/objectives and far more attention to determining his level of functioning. Frequently, their conversations with Roxana touched on the discovery of something else Mark could not do. In time, the teaching team at Ashburn E.S. began to express serious doubts to us at every turn about Mark's ability to live up to the accomplishments demonstrated during first grade at Butterfield School.

On October 26, 1993, Roxana met with Ms. Kelly at the LCPS central office to discuss her perceptions of the staff and concerns related to Mark's educational program. In sum, Roxana was disappointed with Ms. Meadows, the principal at Ashburn E.S. She told Ms. Kelly that Ms. Meadows appeared to have disassociated herself from Mark's inclusion program. Ms. Meadows was ignoring actions needed to solve problems and resolve issues. Further, Roxana said that Ms. Meadows was generally unresponsive to the requests we had made. To us, it was as if Ms. Meadows considered Mark *a special education problem* that she didn't have to address, since she perceived his program as being supervised out of the central office.

To us, the two most important issues requiring immediate action were (1) training for Mark's training assistant (TA) and (2) support for Ms. Jarrett. Roxana asked Ms. Kelly if training was being planned for the TA. Roxana emphasized that the TA had established an effective working relationship with Mark, but did not have a clear idea of how to parlay her relationship into effective support for him in the classroom. From Roxana's classroom observations, the TA stayed in the background, did little parallel teaching, and only stepped in to assist Mark after a task had been levied on the class. This was in significant contrast to Ms. Mrazek's role as Mark's instructional assistant at Butterfield School. Roxana explained that Ms. Mrazek sat next to Mark during class and taught him in parallel using adapted educational materials for each specific lesson, as had been prepared by Ms. Bade, Mark's inclusion facilitator, working from the first-grade teacher's lesson plans.

Concerning curriculum modification for Mark, Roxana expressed concern to Ms. Kelly that Ms. Jarrett was becoming over-stressed, trying to "do it all herself." Roxana urged LCPS to provide Ms. Jarrett with support, someone to adapt the second-grade curriculum to Mark's learning style and abilities. Other issues were also discussed, including the occupational therapist (OT) working with Mark and the need to schedule a consultation with a PE specialist. Finally, Roxana mentioned that Mark's daily schedule was not as consistent as she felt it should be, noting that it was usually prepared after Mark arrived to school. She commented that this was upsetting to Mark and deprived him of the stability in his daily routine that was at the foundation of his success during first grade. Ms. Kelly took detailed notes during their discussion and said that she would follow up on the issues Roxana had identified.

During the school year, regular meetings were held each Wednesday to discuss and propose solutions for any problems encountered by the staff in working with Mark. Normally attending these weekly meetings were Ms. Jarrett, Ms. Conroy-Winters, Ms. Kelly, the TA, Roxana, and Mr. Fred E. Jernigan, a supervisor within LCPS's special education office managing programs for children diagnosed as emotionally disturbed, vision impaired, or with autism. Mr. Jernigan joined the weekly meetings during November 1993, at the request of Ms. Kelly.

At every opportunity during these meetings, Roxana stressed the importance of finding someone to help Ms. Jarrett adapt the school curriculum to best suit Mark's needs. Roxana emphasized her worry that Ms. Jarrett would eventually burn out under the double workload she was carrying if this was not done.

Roxana also raised the issue of training for the TA, time and again referring to it as the "backbone of a successful inclusion program." In one instance, Roxana specifically asked that the TA attend a computer-training course at George Mason University to assist her in working with Mark's educational computer programs. The request was sent to the central office, but was denied: The TA was not a certified elementary teacher and, therefore, was *not eligible* for computer training!

Weeks later, Roxana again raised the need for an adaptive PE consultation. The perceived ambivalence demonstrated by LCPS central office concerning PE was now eroding our confidence in the staff. In a separate conversation, Ms. Meadows told Roxana that she had no control over the matter and that it was out of her hands. She said that decisions concerning Mark's inclusion were being made at the LCPS central office.

Perhaps the most important topic, discussed as early as November 1993 at the weekly meetings, was the emergence of negative behaviors at home, including Mark's use of loud vocal outbursts/sounds and heightened anxiety level. Roxana expressed her deep concern that these behaviors were directly related to the level of frustration Mark was experiencing at school—that this was a definite indicator that all was not well.

On December 20, 1993, we called a meeting with Ms. Meadows and Mr. Dotson, the principal and assistant principal at Ashburn E.S. Here, we presented ourselves as advocates for both Mark *and* for the staff of Ashburn Elementary School. We drove home the point that the staff required professional help—that, without it, the staff was destined for continued frustration over Mark's inclusion program and, eventually, would fail. This directly impacted Mark. We requested Ms. Meadows' support in obtaining the proper resources needed to assist the staff in Mark's inclusion. Ms. Meadows and Mr. Dotson both listened, asked no questions, and said little except to express their empathy. When asked if we should seek an appointment at the central offices of LCPS to discuss these resources, they agreed that it was the logical next step, but appeared apathetic as to whether it would do any good.

Additionally, at this December 20th meeting, Roxana gave Ms. Meadows a document prepared by the Virginia Institute of Developmental Disabilities that outlined the duties and function of an inclusion coordinator. Roxana emphasized the necessity of hiring someone to perform in this capacity for Mark's inclusion. She based her viewpoint on the Butterfield School model, which had proven successful in including Mark. Again, both administrators responded politely, but without any obvious commitment. We simply couldn't understand how any responsible primary school principal could be so complacent, given the circumstances we had outlined. Clearly, Ms. Meadows understood that if LCPS did not take any immediate action, Mark's program would be in jeopardy.

January through May 1994

Early in 1994, we experienced a sharp disagreement with Ms. Jarrett/Ms. Conroy-Winters over Mark's current level of functioning. The current level of functioning document is a narrative description of a child's performance that serves as a baseline for IEP discussions; this document also drives decisions concerning scheduled activities in the child's IEP, as well as the amount of special services required. We judged that Ms. Jarrett/Ms. Conroy-Winters' draft of Mark's level of functioning only highlighted the negative. Therefore, we would not agree with it because we judged that it did not represent a balanced assessment of Mark's academic abilities.

As an alternative, Joseph drafted an assessment document from our perspective and offered it to the Ashburn E.S. staff as a much more accurate portrayal of Mark's performance level. The Ashburn E.S. staff flat out rejected it.

Thereafter, we had one or possibly two meetings with Ms. Jarrett, Ms.

Conroy-Winters, Ms. Meadows, and Mr. Jernigan concerning changes to the draft level of functioning document. These discussions bordered on unreasonable and became increasingly disagreeable. We wondered: *Why is it so important to the staff to diminish Mark's performance on paper in this way?*

Also in early January 1994, Roxana arranged a meeting with Ms. Kelly and Mr. Jernigan at the central offices of LCPS to discuss staff/TA training and the need for an inclusion coordinator to put Mark's inclusion program on solid footing. Roxana also suggested that an education professional with special education experience could be quickly trained to serve as Mark's inclusion coordinator. Passing along the paper describing the role of an inclusion coordinator, Roxana told Ms. Kelly and Mr. Jernigan that we sensed that the Ashburn E.S. staff was burning out and frustrated. Roxana concluded that the staff needed the full support of LCPS administrators—in the form of an inclusion coordinator, at minimum. Both Ms. Kelly and Mr. Jernigan listened. Roxana perceived their response as "polite but bureaucratic." She had pushed for an action plan to be developed, but felt she had received passivity in return.

Roxana asked Ms. Kelly to arrange an appointment with Mr. Neil D. Winters, the director of Pupil Services for LCPS, who was responsible for providing the resources required for special education programs. Days later, Ms. Kelly called Roxana to set the date and time for the meeting.

On January 12th, we met with Mr. Winters at the LCPS central office in Leesburg, Virginia. It was instantly apparent to us that Mr. Winters, as Ms. Conroy-Winters' husband, had detailed knowledge of Mark's placement at Ashburn E.S. We reviewed the issues discussed, days earlier, with Ms. Kelly and Mr. Jernigan. In response, Mr. Winters said plainly that he would *not* have approved Mark's placement as a fully included student in second grade, had he been consulted on the decision. Mr. Winters implied that LCPS had made a significant placement error at the beginning of school, adding that LCPS did not yet have all of the blocks in place to support a fully included student with autism. When we gave Mr. Winters the VIDD outline on the role of an inclusion coordinator, he glanced at it and, upon recognizing what it was, placed it on his desk. Mr. Winters said, flatly, that there was no budget to allow him to hire an inclusion coordinator.

Nonetheless, Mr. Winters asked us to be patient and to work with the staff. He promised that, in time, all of the building blocks would be in place. Concerning the matter of training and adaptive PE, Mr. Winters said that the IEP committee could handle these issues. The meeting ended without pleasantries.

It was readily apparent to us from this short meeting that Mr. Winters was not a proponent of inclusive education. He spoke disparagingly of the experts in education who, he chided, really didn't know anything. Nonetheless, we left the meeting with Mr. Winters feeling that he had spoken honestly. We accepted his proposition to be patient, since Mr. Winters had implied that Mark's placement would not be in jeopardy.

On January 13th, the Eligibility Committee for LCPS met to evaluate the records available on Mark and found that Mark was eligible for special education services. The committee recommended that Mark be identified as a student with autism and speech/language impairments. Further, the Eligibility Committee recommended that the IEP Committee consider additional resources to address the behavioral and academic areas of Mark's program. We noted that our main concerns—training for the staff, curriculum modification assistance for Ms. Jarrett, and an adaptive PE consultation— were never addressed by the Eligibility Committee.

Without knowing it, we were now targeted on LCPS's agenda for dealing with Mark and the inclusion issue. While their agenda had been gaining momentum for weeks, perhaps even months—from our perspective, LCPS did nothing from this point onward to enhance Mark's inclusion program. Everything written, everything spoken was directed toward the same goal: building a credible case for LCPS to prove that Mark was *not able* to learn in a fully inclusive setting, aggressive behaviors and all.

Instead of determining the root cause of Mark's increasingly disturbing behaviors, LCPS quickly moved forward developing a behavior modification plan for Mark. Mr. Fred Jernigan met with the Ashburn E.S. staff on January 25th to outline the behavior plan to be implemented with Mark at school. Included in the behavior plan was a behavior-tracking chart, which would be used to evaluate whether Mark's behaviors were increasing or decreasing in frequency. Ms. Conroy-Winters and Ms. Jarrett wrote a memorandum for the record concerning their meeting with Mr. Jernigan. Although they sent us a copy, including a sample of the chart that would be used to track Mark's aggressive behaviors, by the time we were notified, the whole behavior plan was presented to us as a *fait accompli*. We also noted that this memorandum was the only one that we ever received from either Ms. Conroy-Winters or Ms. Jarrett. This appeared most unusual to us.

In early February 1994, Ms. Jamie Ruppmann, an educational expert who had been a consultant to LCPS, evaluated Mr. Jernigan's behavior plan. She noted that Mark did "not see snack food as a behavior contingent re-enforcer." While the use of M&Ms as a re-enforcer came to an end, the charting continued unabated at school. Only then did it become evident to us that the real importance in all of this was *the charting activity.* There was no doubt in our minds, then, that the behavior plan had but one purpose: to amass evidence on the frequency and intensity of Mark's aggressive behaviors at school.

The second-quarter grading period reports prepared by Ms. Jarrett and Ms. Conroy-Winters in early February, 1994, are interesting, given their contrast with the first quarter reports. In her second-quarter report, Ms. Jarrett wrote that "he may not understand what is being read or perhaps he is not reading the stories as independently as I had hoped."

Further, Ms. Jarrett wrote, "It continues to be difficult to assess Mark's mathematical abilities. He has done some programs on the computer with a great deal of success. He is particularly successful with Counting Critters. This is a pre-kindergarten program designed to help students count several objects."

It is interesting and curious how Ms. Jarrett praises Mark in her report for the work he has done in music and in art: "Mark loves music. He claps to the beat and will play instruments if given the opportunity and help. He listens to and follows direction." And, "Art is a positive experience for Mark. He participates well, although he consistently needs to play with a particular stuffed animal." It is important to note here that the perception among primary school teachers, at the time, was that "special education children" could only be "mainstreamed" in art and music—both nonacademic classes.

Ms. Conroy-Winters also wrote a second-quarter grading period report for Mark. Similar to Ms. Jarrett's report, Ms. Conroy-Winters' report contrasts sharply with her report at the end of the first quarter. It is also noted that Ms. Conroy-Winters is identified as the case manager for Mark, on this report. Her close ties to Mark as his speech pathologist and case manager, however, would soon become more distant.

In her second quarter grading report, Ms. Conroy-Winters wrote, "The question continues to arise about how much Mark is really reading and understanding." And, "without facilitated communication (FC) we have not been able to get him to answer any questions on the Canon, even when given the answer verbally." While we challenged these reports, the answers we were given never reconciled the stark differences noted between the first and second quarter grading periods.

Next came the IEP meetings. The IEP meetings held on February 17th and February 28th were "truly contentious," in our opinion. By mid-winter 1994, the Ashburn E.S. staff had buried any pretense of civility toward us. They simply were not reasonable during these discussions. We saw the current level of functioning (CLF) document as cast from a negative viewpoint, too harsh, lacking balance, and not at all representative of our baseline, holistic picture of Mark. We could not, and would not, accept the school's CLF draft. In addition, we were both greatly frustrated, dealing with the principal.

Nonetheless, during the IEP meeting on February 17th, Mr. Fred Jernigan (who now replaced Ms. Kelly on the IEP team) recommended that Ms. Valerie Mason, a special education teacher, be involved in Mark's program for three hours per week as a resource consultant to Mark's teachers. We agreed with Mr. Jernigan's recommendation and signed an IEP document to make it happen. This was now the second time that LCPS had acted to ostensibly show its good will and to demonstrate its support of Mark's inclusion program. Even though Ms. Mason's presence on Mark's IEP team was non-essential, we judged the recommendation as sincere.

Prior to the IEP meeting planned for March 18th, we prepared two documents to share with the Ashburn E.S. staff. We hoped that these documents would iron out differences regarding Mark's current level of functioning and lead to a draft that we could endorse. These two documents entitled, "Ideas to be considered in the IEP for Mark A. Hartmann," and "Present Level of Functioning," demonstrated how frustrated we were in working with the staff at Ashburn E.S.

The IEP meeting on March 18, 1994, was interesting on several levels. First, we were asked to sign the IEP with the following statement noted in script: "The eligibility committee found Mark to be eligible for services as an autistic student with the related services of speech/language and occupational therapy. The attached goals and objectives will be worked on until June 1994. The IEP committee agrees that these are appropriate at this time." Since IEPs are usually developed to cover a full year beginning with the next academic year, when we questioned the IEPs end date of June 1994 (just two and a half months from the date of this IEP meeting), the principal explained that all IEPs are reviewed at the end of the year, as standard procedure. Being naive, we believed her, not wanting to think that there was a hidden agenda at work here.

Unfortunately, our faith in Ms. Meadows was misplaced. The truth was that IEPs in Loudoun County are reviewed and signed on an annual basis unless the parents call for an earlier IEP meeting to address a specific issue. Thus, Mark's IEP should have been dated March 1994 to March 1995; the hand scripted note calling for a June 1994 conclusion was markedly out of the norm. Perhaps we should have intuited that they only planned to commit to inclusive schooling for Mark through June of that year. For as soon as Mark's IEP document was signed, the Ashburn E.S. staff appeared to gloat, as if to say, "We won!" Little did we know, Ashburn E.S. would soon recommend that Mark be transferred out of their school altogether, to a segregated program for children with autism held at Leesburg E.S.

At this same meeting, Mr. Jernigan expressed doubt that Mark's program would succeed. Joseph stopped Mr. Jernigan in his tracks and asked him to explain what he meant. After Mr. Jernigan attempted to explain, an attempt that further infuriated us both, Joseph asked point blank, "Tell me now—who is accountable and responsible for the success of Mark's inclusion program?" To our dismay, no one said a word! The Ashburn E.S. staff sat there motionless and totally speechless. As a supervisory representative from LCPS's special education office, a replacement for Ms. Kelly, and Mark's former "acting inclusion coordinator," Mr. Jernigan also remained silent. Joseph asked again, and then again, the same question, *"Who is accountable and responsible for the success of Mark's inclusion program?"* After a long, continued silence, the principal of Ashburn E.S., Ms. Meadows, finally responded and took responsibility for Mark's program. Now the picture was clearing! Joseph's response was swift, "That's big of you to step forward and be accountable. Why did it take so long for you to decide?" There was no answer. This was the height of Ms. Meadows' disingenuousness!

Given this turn of events and the fact that we could no longer trust Ms. Meadows, we came close to negating the IEP that we had just signed. As doing so might be considered a hostile act, however, we chose to take no immediate action. As it later turned out, our conciliatory nature played into LCPS's plot against us.

The truth of the matter was, it was us, *Mark's parents,* who had been the ones working at a fever's pitch to ensure the success of Mark's inclusion program. Ms. Meadows and her staff were always placating, *but not acting* to ensure the success of Mark's inclusion program. This was "passive–aggressive" behavior at its very worst!

A few days after the IEP meeting, Joseph sat down with Ms. Jarrett and Ms. Conroy-Winters to negotiate a current level of functioning document acceptable to both sides. This document would be included with the recently signed IEP. A compromise had to be made, as the teachers seemed driven to get a baseline that was not at all flattering for Mark. Although we did not fully agree with the final, negotiated document, Joseph just wanted to get on with the process and move beyond Mark's initial IEP in Loudoun County. After all, it was now mid-March, and there were only two months of school remaining for second grade. We wanted to focus LCPS on the preparations necessary for Mark's third grade inclusion placement. We simply wanted to avoid at all costs what had happened to Mark in second grade!

On March 24th, we met with Mr. Edward B. Hamilton, superintendent of Loudoun County Public Schools, to discuss Mark's placement at Ashburn E.S. as a fully included student. We briefed Mr. Hamilton on the successful two years of inclusive education in Lombard, Illinois, prior to our move to Loudoun County. Roxana raised the issue of staff training at Ashburn E.S., describing it as wholly inadequate, as well as the absolute, essential need for an inclusion facilitator to be hired to assist the staff. Mr. Hamilton responded that he was aware of Mark's placement and accepted the premise that it would be unfair to judge the success of Mark's placement without the appropriate resources being put into place. We invited Mr. Hamilton to visit Mark's classroom and to become personally involved in acquiring the needed resources. Mr. Hamilton did not respond to this invitation. The meeting with Mr. Hamilton could only be characterized as stiff, formal, and all business, with little empathy expressed toward us as parents, or for the circumstances we faced. To us, he appeared to be a cold-hearted bureaucrat who had little interest in parents, children, or in solving the educational challenges posed by his programs.

At the end of March, Ms. Jarrett, Ms. Conroy-Winters, and Ms. Mason submitted Mark's third quarter grading reports. In those reports, Ms. Mason was now listed as replacing Ms. Conroy-Winters as Mark's case manager. This struck us as odd because, as just a "part time" consultant to the school, Ms. Mason was now listed as "program manager." It also stuck us as odd because we were never notified of the switch in roles, nor did the reports highlight this change. To reiterate, Ms. Mason, who joined Mark's IEP team in February, 1994, as a three-hour-per-week special education consultant, was now, a month later in March, 1994, Mark's *program manager*.

In looking back, having Ms. Mason as Mark's program manager was an important stratagem for LCPS because she held special education credentials. Secondly, we suspect that LCPS wanted to distance Ms. Conroy-Winters from a position of responsibility concerning Mark's inclusion program. After all, it would not look good in court for the wife of Mr. Neil Winters to be so closely involved with a contentious special education issue involving inclusion!

Overall, LCPS staff reported a continuing decline in Mark's academic and behavioral conduct at school during their third-quarter grading period reports. In her report, Ms. Jarrett wrote, "Mark has been unable to show that he is reading or comprehending many of the stories being read." Again, this is a big difference compared to her first quarter report on Mark's reading abilities.

Ms. Jarrett also wrote that Mark's mathematical abilities were difficult to assess, but again mentioned that he could accomplish the pre-kindergarten computer program *Counting Critters* with a great deal of success. Although couched as a positive, this statement identified Mark as performing two years below grade level.

Finally, Ms. Jarrett wrote, "I continue to see Mark become frustrated in many activities. As a result, he continues to bite, shriek, pinch, kick, and cry during the day. I believe much of this behavior is the result of the academic gap between Mark, who appears to be on the pre-K level, and the rest of the class as they begin to prepare for more independent work that will be required of them in third grade."

Concerning reading, Ms. Mason wrote, "During teaching sessions, Mark is able to attend to task for 3-5 minutes."

In her third-quarter report, Ms. Mason also wrote, "The focus of individual teaching sessions has been to establish Mark's current levels of functioning in math and reading and to develop new math and reading skills." Can you imagine! This occurred over a period of just seven weeks of evaluation.

Ms. Conroy-Winters titled her report, "Current Level of Functioning." This *speech pathologist,* wrote, "Academically, Mark is working on his own individual objectives, as the second grade curriculum appears too difficult for him."

Regarding reading, Ms. Conroy-Winters wrote, "Mark appears to be at the pre-reading level." She also wrote, "In Math, Mark can match sets of objects to the number representing them up to five."

In addition, Ms. Conroy-Winters wrote, "Mark continues to use behaviors such as hitting, kicking or pinching to communicate negative responses, although this is happening less frequently since appropriate objectives have been established."

Finally, she wrote, "Socially, Mark has difficulty interacting with his peers."

This last comment and similar comments made by Ms. Jarrett more adequately describe Mark's disability: Autism. Because he remained disabled and continued to display behavioral traits typical of autism, this was deemed "negative" in their minds and became dominant as they described Mark in their third-quarter reports. We judged that it was this errant attitude that led these teachers to conclude that Mark was not profiting from being fully included in the second grade classroom. We also knew that the third quarter grading report written by Ms. Conroy-Winters contrasted sharply with the observations that she'd written about in her first grading period report. Nonetheless, we agreed that, indeed, there had been regression in Mark's educational program. We judged, however, that Mark's regression was due largely to the way the Ashburn E.S. staff had approached his inclusion.

By the time May 1994 arrived, we were just trying to survive the year intact. From Illinois to Northern Virginia, we had suffered a bewildering difference in educational approaches over the past year and were alarmed by the negative effects that this was having on Mark. Hoping for a different outcome in Virginia, we invited Ms. Kenna Colley, an inclusion specialist from the Gilbert Linkous Elementary School in Blacksburg, Virginia, to observe Mark in his Ashburn E.S. classroom. After receiving our written request, Ms.

Meadows gave permission for Ms. Colley to visit Mark's classroom on June 10, 1994, during the last week of school.

On May 15th, we sent another letter to Ms. Meadows identifying all of the issues that needed to be addressed at the upcoming, end-of-year IEP meeting. These issues included: (1) summer program for Mark, (2) planning for the 1994-95 school year, (3) invitation for the third-grade teacher to participate in the IEP meeting, and (4) an adaptive physical education program.

The IEP meeting was set for May 31, 1994. Initially, Ms. Meadows ignored the issues raised in our letter. When Roxana called to discuss the matter, Ms. Meadows said that with the exception of selecting Mark's third grade teacher, all of the other issues were to be handled by various functionaries within LCPS; she maintained that the other issues would have to be handled separately from the scheduled IEP meeting. Dissatisfied with this response, Roxana hand-carried a letter to LCPS superintendent, Mr. Hamilton, requesting his intervention to ensure that all appropriate decision-makers would be in attendance at Mark's IEP meeting. There was no response.

CHAPTER 9

PERCEPTIONS
1994

During the IEP meeting in late May, a new element in Ms. Jarrett's annual report bothered us greatly. Her comments about Mark's behaviors were nothing short of alarming! Ms. Jarrett wrote, "Mark has shown extreme aggressive behavior to adults working with him and the children in the classroom. At times, this has been a dangerous situation for the other students. As Mark grows and becomes stronger, it is more difficult to stop this behavior."

While believing that Ms. Jarrett's statement was filled with extravagant exaggeration at best, we decided that it was worth our effort to get to the truth. We sent a letter to the family of each child in Mark's second grade class, including a survey for the parents to complete with their child's input. The focus of the survey was Mark's behavior at school.

Dated July 2, 1994, the cover letter read, in part:

> This year in second grade at Ashburn E.S. was a challenge for all concerned because Mark Hartmann was the first disabled student to be fully integrated with peers in Loudoun County. While we did well this year, we feel that many areas need to be improved, not just for Mark, but also for all of the children who will be in class with him. Our focus is to advocate for Mark and for all of the students and teachers who will come into contact with Mark daily during the school year. As you may know, Mark is the first student with a severe communication disorder to be placed into a regular second-grade class in Loudoun County. As such, and in an effort to advocate effectively for our son, we have developed the attached survey that we are asking all parents to complete. At the end of the survey, we have included a comment section. Please feel confident to mention

both the positive and negative aspects of your child's experience with Mark, as well as your own.

There were eleven questions in all for the parents of the twenty-one students in Mark's class. We provided ample space on the survey for answers and comments:

1. Is Mark the first person with a disability that you have come to know either personally or through your child?
2. How many other disabled people do you know?
3. Were you surprised that Mark was included in the regular second grade classroom? Write any thoughts on your initial reaction.
4. How often did you spend time in the classroom during the school year? Number of visits?
5. Did your child ever talk to you about Mark? Please provide any specific comments.
6. Did your child have any unpleasant interactions with Mark? Write any comments.
7. Do you judge that your child is now more aware of disabilities, both physical and neurological, than before school began with Mark in the classroom? If yes, are there any other benefits incurred to your child? Please explain.
8. Has Mark's inclusion in the second grade classroom had any effect on your child's educational performance? If yes, please explain.
9. Did your child participate in any after-school activities with Mark, such as birthday parties, sleep over parties, or sports activities?
10. Do you want your child to share the same classroom with Mark next year? Any comments?
11. As a parent, would you be willing to share your experience and views about Mark during group meetings with parents with disabled children in Loudoun County? Any comments?

In an addendum, we posed some questions to the students themselves and addressed the issue of Mark's communication disorder:

He makes all kinds of vocal sounds to express his mood. Some of these noises are alarming to the unprepared or untrained person, especially the first time Mark acts out in frustration. Within a very short time, however, it is common to become familiar with Mark's vocal sounds and to identify the meaning of most of them.... Please ask your child to comment on Mark's vocal sounds during class.

  1. Were you able to tune Mark's noises out?
  2. Did you look at Mark a lot during class?
  3. Did you learn to interpret Mark's sounds?
  4. Was the presence of a teacher's aide for Mark reassuring for you, that someone was there to care for Mark and look after his needs?

Thirteen parents responded. Their written comments included the following:

At first I was surprised that he was there, and my daughter's early comments about him worried me - that Mark might disrupt the class. But I soon quit worrying about that. My daughter adjusted to it and he just became part of the class to her.... Once Mark inadvertently kicked our daughter in the head while the class was in the reading corner. She understood he didn't mean it, but it hurt her.... There were times when my daughter felt a little frustrated by the speed the lessons went, but I'm not convinced that was Mark's fault. She is exceptionally bright and I believe most of the problem was that her boredom at times caused her to become a little lazy. She also mentioned once or twice that the sounds Mark makes occasionally disrupted her concentration - but the times I was in the classroom, I observed that the class got along quite well with him there.... Mark's assistant did a wonderful job with him, keeping him focused and thereby allowing the class to proceed and him to go with them. I feel that a full-time assistant is necessary in his case, or the teacher ends up spending too much time on him..., then I feel the class suffers.

~~~~~~

I think it's wonderful. It gives children the idea that people with disabilities are not people they should be afraid of.... Sometimes Mark would hit other children or pinch cheeks to get their attention. My son learned about how hard it is for some people to communicate and how not to be angered by this disability. He learned how to tell what Mark was feeling (angry, happy, frustrated) by his expressions and his movements.

~~~~~~

He would always tell me about Mark and the things that would make him happy. He was thrilled to see any of Mark's accomplishments and would comment about them quite frequently. He loved to see Mark laugh.

~~~~~~

I was not surprised (at Mark's inclusion). I didn't think it was unusual. My daughter likes Mark. He is friendly. I explained to my daughter that Mark couldn't talk out loud as others, but used the computer to communicate. She did comment that there were occasional vocal outbursts, but that it did not interfere with the learning environment.... I think she has a better understanding of what a disability is and that a disabled person is capable of doing comparable work.

~~~~~~

Our only negative experience with Mark came the first day of school. My son came home with tears in his eyes. I knew he had been nervous about going to a new school, and not knowing anyone in his classroom.... The day had gone well, except for one "big kid" who had yelled loudly and had kicked his feet. My son was afraid of Mark. He said the yelling scared him, and he didn't understand why Mark didn't stop yelling or why the teacher didn't ask him to stop.... I still think my child is a little afraid of Mark, and I feel that may well stem from his first impression.... Please ask the teacher to explain to her class about Mark in children's terms on the first day or maybe have Mark and his parents come the second day of school so that there can be time to get to know Mark after that first day is over.... The teacher spoke to my son (and I think the whole class) on the second day of school, and he came home happy.

~~~~~~

At the beginning of the year my daughter explained to us what she thought autism was and had some questions about it. Throughout the year she mentioned Mark once in a while but usually in a positive way. She never made any negative comments regarding Mark or having him in the classroom.... I think that this experience gave her a better appreciation of how lucky she is and developed more compassion for children with disabilities. She did very well in second grade and seemed to be able to do her work without any problem. I think the teacher did an exceptional job of handling the classroom with Mark in it. I'm not sure all teachers could do it.... I have been out of the special education field for several years now but professionally, I feel that Mark would benefit more from a classroom for children with communication disorders in which he would receive intensive therapy. I understand the value of normal peer role models for disabled children and could see that helping Mark on a part-time basis, maybe half-day mainstreaming into a regular classroom. I also have concerns that, as Mark becomes bigger and stronger, he will be more difficult to handle and much more disruptive to a classroom and possibly physically harmful.

~~~~~~

Mark hit my son once, then indicated he was sorry and my son was not at all upset by the incident. He thinks Mark just wanted to be left alone…. The ability of the children to accept Mark in their circle was a wonderful thing to witness. I hope that will remain true as Mark gets older…. This experience brought out some very good qualities in my son: patience, understanding, and cooperation.

~~~~~~

My son was very interested in Mark and liked him very much. Mark had a very positive effect on my son. I hope he will be in future classes with him. Mark is a great asset to the second graders. It taught my son that people with a disability have some restrictions but all in all they are people, too. They also can be great friends. That is what Mark is to my son…. My son saw that Mark had a disability and tried very hard to succeed. In turn, my son tried very hard to complete things that were tough for him…. Mark is a wonderful, happy person. I have had the pleasure of meeting Mark and his parents. They do wonderful things for Mark and I hope the school will make it easy on them to continue.

~~~~~~

I think my child has grown emotionally by having Mark as a friend. I saw a compassionate, caring side of my child I didn't know existed. I think at the second-grade level, children should be exposed to all types of children whether it is difference of race, color, religion or handicap. Children are unbiased at this age and they need to realize that the world is made up of different kinds of people and that we can all live and learn together in harmony.

The children's responses were equally comprehensive and varied. Ten of the thirteen responding children said they were able to tune out Mark's vocal sounds; three said they were sometimes able. Four children admitted that they did look at Mark a lot during class; four others said they did not. Three children said sometimes, and two indicated "not so much."

Six children said they could understand Mark's vocal sounds and one said he could understand with the help of Mark's body language. Two children said they "sometimes" understood Mark, while two more answered they understood "some of" Mark's vocalizations. Of the thirteen children responding, only three indicated they were unable to interpret Mark's vocal sounds.

Unanimously, the children who responded reported that the presence of an aide was reassuring. One parent chose to use a direct quote from his child: "When you get to know somebody who isn't quite that same as you, it doesn't mean that you don't enjoy being around him. Mark is my friend."

Tears came to our eyes reading these responses! These comments, as written by parents and children in Mark's class, came from the heart and were honest. For a change, Mark was recognized for his wonderful inherent qualities and not disparaged by people constantly evaluating him through the prism of prejudice and stereotype. Without knowing that a controversy was brewing over Mark's inclusion in Loudoun County, the parents of Mark's second grade classmates had given their candid views. As it was, these parents/children were *far different* from the LCPS professionals who were driven by hidden agendas and harboring ulterior motives. The results of the survey spoke volumes of reassurance to us, as parents.

LCPS - Obstinate over Extended School Year Services

Following the May 31st IEP meeting portrayed in the first chapter of this book, the working relationship between Roxana and Ashburn E.S. deteriorated quickly. Whereas LCPS agreed to provide Mark with a summer program involving one hour of speech/language therapy, in-home, each day for four weeks, it refused our plea to assign someone other than Ms. Conroy-Winters as Mark's therapist.

We felt pressured by LCPS to accept these conditions. If we wanted a summer speech program for Mark, it would have to be with Ms. Conroy-Winters. If we refused her, then there would be no LCPS-sponsored summer program for Mark, period. Despite the pressure, in the end, we decided *not* to accept Ms. Conroy-Winters under any circumstances.

Due to our growing distrust of LCPS even well before the May 31st IEP meeting, Roxana began looking for non-Loudoun County teachers to work with Mark on a private-hire basis. She eventually contacted Ms. Cathy Thornton, a special education teacher from Fairfax County, and made arrangements for her to work with Mark two hours a day, three days a week, beginning in mid-May, 1994. Ms. Thornton had eleven years of experience teaching children with autism and quickly established a wonderful working relationship with Mark.

During the weeks that followed, Ms. Thornton increased Mark's time on task from an average of ten minutes to thirty minutes without any serious behavior problems. In several instances, Ms. Thornton was able to get Mark to stay on task for forty-five minutes! Roxana noticed that Ms. Thornton used a lot of reading materials with Mark and, through the use of books on taped cassette, reintroduced Mark to the enjoyment of reading—just like he had experienced at Butterfield School in Lombard, Illinois. We were overjoyed with the results of Ms. Thornton's efforts with Mark! She renewed our belief that the problems experienced during Mark's LCPS inclusion program were not exclusively of Mark's making. Her experience with Mark provided yet another invaluable perspective.

An Independent Viewpoint

Then, on June 10th, Ms. Kenna Colley visited Ashburn E.S. as planned, to observe Mark in his second-grade classroom. As a special education teacher and inclusion specialist from Blacksburg, Virginia (Montgomery County), we had asked Ms. Colley to provide insights on Mark's current program and suggestions on how to improve it. She spent approximately four hours observing Mark during his morning schedule.

Following her observation visit, Ms. Colley wrote a detailed report recognizing Ms. Jarrett as an effective teacher and offering a list of suggestions to improve Mark's inclusion program. Training the staff on autism and facilitated communication, providing assistance with curriculum modifications, and peer training were all high on Ms. Colley's list. The following general observations are quoted from Ms. Colley's report:

1. Mark was well liked by peers in his classroom. They appeared to want to interact and spend time with him.
2. Mark followed directions very well. Yet, he experienced difficulty with transitions that were not well communicated to him, or during transitions from break to work situations.
3. Mark had a fairly good relationship with the instructional assistant. She had minimal interactions with other students and was required to stay primarily with Mark throughout the day.
4. The communications board was a good method for Mark to communicate quickly and effectively. He needed an additional augmentative system to further elaborate communication choices and ideas.
5. Mark is a child with autism that needs to be valued the way he is.

Autism will always be a part of him and his unique characteristics need to be accepted by all members of an educational team, and educational approaches need to emphasize his strengths and abilities.

6. Mark was provided with excellent role models by being with his same age peers without disabilities. He imitated their general behaviors and he needed this constant input to learn to socialize within our society.

7. Mark's educational team appeared to have had to learn to include him with little training. A cohesive approach was not evident.

8. I did not observe any forceful or aggressive tendencies in Mark. He appeared to be a gentle boy who was frustrated by transitions and change. He did not appear to put himself or his classmates in any kind of danger.

9. I was not aware of any consistent behavior strategies being implemented at school. Most team members did not appear to be aware of a behavior plan or of its existence.

10. Mark did not interfere with the learning of other students in his class and was not disruptive to the overall class routine.

In addition, Ms. Colley supplied the following written suggestions, recommending the use of a team approach to successfully include Mark in third grade for the 1994-95 school year:

1. The staff/team needs resources and information on what autism is. Persons with autism are people who need to be in so-called "normal" environments to learn and interact with peers around them. I suggest reading books written by persons with autism and reading RECENT literature that includes facilitated communication techniques, information on movement and sensory disorders, and best practices for teaching persons with autism.

2. Classroom lessons should be adapted on a weekly basis based on the general education teacher's lesson plans. An inclusion specialist or facilitator must be assigned to Mark's team to provide training to the instructional assistant and classroom teacher and other team members. This person should also be responsible for making adaptations and accommodations to the general education curriculum and working with the team and the parents to identify and prioritize objectives that are

important for Mark. This person must be knowledgeable about best practices in inclusion and have a good knowledge about persons with autism.

3. Monthly team meetings are suggested that include the parents to discuss Mark's progress and ongoing educational services. There should be a specific form used to indicate what the issues are at each meeting, what action will be taken for each issue, and who is responsible for carrying out these actions. This provides documentation for each meeting and is a quick visual assessment of what has been accomplished as the year progresses.

4. Peer planning and support sessions need to be conducted with Mark's classmates to provide them with honest information regarding his needs and to teach them strategies to interact with him and help establish friendships.

5. A specific plan for behavioral concerns needs to be in place and used consistently by all team members. This obviously will be based on non-aversive techniques that closely resemble the techniques used with Mark's classmates. The plan needs to be created and agreed upon by all team members; not established by an outsider who does not know Mark and his needs on a daily basis.

6. Training for all team members in facilitated communication techniques. Additional training may be provided in areas of need, i.e., how to best utilize an instructional assistant within a classroom, etc. This may include observations in other school divisions.

7. The Loudoun County team that was trained in non-aversive behavior techniques should provide consults. This training was offered in 1992-93 through a state-funded program. The special education director (Ms. Kelly) would be able to identify the county personnel who have received this training.

8. Provide Mark with a daily picture schedule at his desk to help with transitions. He needs to have some way to have more choice making and control within his schedule and have a systematic way of checking off when time periods are over.

9. A portfolio assessment is recommended to maintain continuous documentation of Mark's progress. This may include videotapes of him across the school day, work samples, peer feedback, and other relative pieces of information that can provide educational teams with needed information year to year.

10. The occupational therapist may want to periodically observe Mark at different parts of his school day to make recommendations to the educational team on how to implement sensory integration techniques into his school day.
11. Mark may want to begin remaining at school for lunch with his peers since this is a very social time of the day and he could benefit from these interactions. Maybe a break could be put into his schedule after lunch if he needs some quiet time or some personal space after a very active day.
12. Increasing Mark's academic skills and length of time engaged in them appears to be necessary. Mark is an intelligent child who will benefit from more direct instruction. He appears to have a high receptive ability. There is a saying, "Just because a person cannot talk does not mean they have nothing to say." I think this holds true for Mark; he cannot be adequately assessed due to his limited expressive communicative abilities.

We felt so *heard* and *validated* following Ms. Colley's visit—as if she understood our son's challenges with autism and what was needed from the school system to return him to the success he'd experienced in a fully included learning environment, as at Butterfield School. Ms. Colley's consultative report hit home on several fronts. It reflected many of the same ideas and concerns that we had raised, time and time again, with Ms. Meadows and other LCPS administrators during Mark's second grade year. Her observations of Mark as a gentle person were particularly insightful and paralleled our own view of Mark. Ms. Colley understood that Mark's perceived "behaviors" were the communicative expressions of a boy frustrated by transitions and change, not dangerous acts of aggression in themselves.

Ms. Colley's report, of course, clashed significantly with the statements read by the Ashburn E.S. staff at the May 31st IEP meeting. It seemed clear to us that the LCPS teachers/staff were, at best, misinterpreting Mark's behaviors, as they lacked the insight and perspective that comes with sufficient autism-related training/experience. Furthermore, it also occurred to us that their use of behavior charts and negative representation of Mark's behaviors seemed calculated and devised specifically to support their hidden agenda.

Leesburg Autism Program

Just days after Ms. Colley's visit, on June 15, 1994, Roxana visited the segregated classroom for children with autism at Leesburg Elementary School in Loudoun County, Virginia. Ashburn E.S. was recommending that Mark be placed in this program for his third-grade year.

While observing the class at Leesburg E.S., Roxana noted the absence of an augmentative communication system in use for any of the children; the wide difference in age among the three children; and, the scarcity of decorations in the room compared to the numerous, colorful decorations observed in other classrooms. Overall, Roxana judged that the environment was *not* one that would benefit Mark, given his level of awareness and ability to follow a regular classroom schedule of activities. Furthermore, Leesburg Elementary School was more than ten miles from our home in Ashburn. After visiting the program at Leesburg E.S., Roxana concluded that this segregated placement would not benefit Mark…educationally, socially, or communicatively.

CHAPTER 10

WAITING TO BE SUED
1994

G iven the certainty of imminent legal action, we hired an attorney from Herndon, Virginia, who specialized in special education law to represent Mark's interests. During our initial talks, Mr. Gerard "Jerry" S. Rugel spoke with uncommon frankness and honesty. He advised us not to fight LCPS over Mark's educational placement for third grade, but rather to move to another school district that would provide Mark with a fully inclusive education.

After reviewing the laws applicable to our circumstance, we were nonetheless convinced that we were on the right side of the issue and decided to stay the course. Mr. Rugel was thorough, compassionate, patient, and understanding in representing us. He carefully introduced us to the complexities of special education law and the precedent-setting cases that we would encounter along our legal path. At the same time, he quickly absorbed the details of Mark's educational history and the circumstances experienced during the school year at Ashburn E.S.

On June 27, 1994, Roxana received a letter written by LCPS's Director of Special Education, Ms. Kelly, dated June 24. The letter began, "The purpose of this letter is to notify you that I have initiated a due process appeal *on behalf of your son, Mark,* with respect to issues relating to his special education placement status." In essence, LCPS had initiated legal action to resolve their dispute with us regarding Mark's educational placement in public school. While the first step in due process is normally "mediation"—i.e., between parents and school district—LCPS decided to bypass mediation altogether, opting instead to file a legal suit against us, as parents. While LCPS alleged that they were "acting on behalf of our son," in fact, this was their first step toward placing Mark in a segregated educational program—against our wishes and better judgment. Little did we know that this letter would launch the legal battle that would dominate our lives for the next four years.

We particularly resented the wording of the text, even though Ms. Kelly's letter was little more than pro-forma. It was as if LCPS had established itself as the authority, taking necessary action to protect Mark from the misjudgments of his parents. We viewed this letter as a demonstration of power and position, even as an attempt to intimidate. The letter also announced that "the Supreme Court of Virginia had appointed Ms. Nancy A. McBride of Alexandria to serve as Hearing Officer in this case." Ms. McBride subsequently arranged for the due process hearing to begin on August 15, 1994.

Prior to the start of the due process hearing, we pressed LCPS for the extended school year services outlined in Mark's IEP. Mark was to receive four weeks of speech/language therapy during the summer, beginning July 5th, at five hours per week. We formally noted our objection to the assignment of Ms. Conroy-Winters as Mark's summer speech/language therapist because she would surely be called as a primary witness against us in the due process hearing. In closing a letter to LCPS dated July 1st, we wrote, "Given the situation, it is inconceivable that you would hold Mark's extended year services hostage to obtain our agreement to allow Ms. Conroy-Winters to enter our home on a daily basis. We respectfully request that you reconsider your position in this matter and select another staff person to provide Mark with the communication services which are his right under the Individuals with Disabilities Education Act (IDEA) per the unanimous recommendation of his IEP Team." Joseph faxed the letter to Ms. Kelly the same day it was written.

In a last ditch effort to resolve the matter, Ms. Jaime Ruppmann (the education consultant who was helping us) spoke with Ms. Kelly later that same day, imploring her to find an alternative to Ms. Conroy-Winters, as we had requested. Ms. Kelly responded that she would discuss the matter with Mr. Winters over the weekend for a final decision.

On Monday morning at 6:00 a.m., Ms. Ruppmann received a call from Mr. Winters. He directed Ms. Ruppmann to call the LCPS lawyer, Ms. Mehfoud, for a response to our letter. When Ms. Ruppmann placed the call to Ms. Mehfoud's office, she was told that Ms. Mehfoud was on vacation and would not be back in the office until the following week.

The response from LCPS finally came from Mr. Fred Jernigan in a letter dated July 5th. He wrote, "We've heard your objections to having Ms. Conroy-Winters provide these services, but continue to feel that she clearly is the most appropriate person to implement this extended year IEP." In the end, we were powerless to oppose LCPS's will. LCPS was interested in being neither reasonable nor fair in its dealings with us. The heated tension between LCPS and us had increased to near-fever pitch by this point.

Preparatory Evaluations

To prepare for the legal proceedings ahead, our attorney, Mr. Rugel, advised that we have Mark evaluated by several professionals outside the LCPS system. We would spend the next month arranging for OT and academic evaluations, including the results from a former intelligence test.

On June 9, 1994, Ms. Myra Smith Beckler, an occupational therapist from Fairfax County, completed the OT evaluation of Mark we requested. In her summary, Ms. Beckler wrote:

> Mark is a loveable young boy who is experiencing many difficulties in processing sensory information associated with neurological abnormalities typical of autism. Difficulties with modulation of sensory input are observed especially in the tactile, vestibular, and proprioceptive systems. Mark has not mastered many gross motor, fine motor, and visual perceptive tasks in spite of the effort and energy put forth to develop these skills. Mark's tactile system does not appear to be well regulated, especially with temperature sensation. Mark has demonstrated the ability to understand directions, motor-plan test items, and to complete tasks. He uses non-verbal communication and gestures to indicate his needs. Testing results on a visual motor test at 5 years 2 months and on a visual perception test of 4 years 9 months are indicative of higher cognitive functioning.

Ms. Beckler's evaluative mention of "higher cognitive functioning" reminded us of similar results when, in May 1992, Mark had been given the Test of Non-verbal Intelligence (TONI-2 Test). The TONI-2 evaluation was completed by the director of the Center for the Study of Autism, Inc., who was visiting Chicago from Portland, Oregon. Mark scored an IQ of 111 on the test. Mark's eight-year-old sister, Laura, also took the TONI-2 test and scored an IQ of 109. Both scores were in the average intelligence range.

Also in June 1994, we asked Ms. Cathy A. Thornton, M.A. to evaluate Mark's academic abilities using the Woodcock-Johnson Tests of Achievement (WJ-R). This would provide standardized test results independent of those obtained by LCPS teachers/staff, as needed to characterize Mark's academic skills and behaviors. We also knew that Ms. Thornton had developed a wonderful working relationship with Mark and that the report would carry weight in court when presented as documentary evidence, supported by her testimony as a special education teacher.

Ms. Thornton conducted her evaluation of Mark at home on June 28th, June 30th, July 1st, and July 12th, 1994. The following passages are excerpted from Ms. Thornton's "Report of Educational Evaluation" of Mark:

- (Standard scores on the WJ-R are based on a mean score of 100). Mark received a Standard Score (SS) of 79 on the Broad Reading Cluster. The two sub-tests that comprise this cluster are Letter-Word (L-W) Identification (SS=82, Age Equivalent 7-6, 11%) and Passage Comprehension (SS=80, Age Equivalent 7-2, 9%). Basal limits were obtained on both of these sub-tests. Ms. Thornton provided physical support to Mark (facilitation) under his arm throughout the evaluation sessions.

- The Broad Math Cluster was given on another day. The sub-tests in this cluster are Calculation (SS=33, Age Equivalent 5-9, .1%) and Applied Problems (SS=48, Age Equivalent 4-5, .1%). Mark's Standard Score on this cluster was 32. This was the day that Mark was congested and given medication. He became very silly, laughing and moving around a great deal. Basals were not obtained on these two sub-tests.

- Informal observations: Mark has improved in his ability to work for extended periods of time (30 - 45 minutes), responding very appropriately to the use of a kitchen timer to remain at the work table, and to return to the table when cued by the bell. There are times that he understandably becomes frustrated, however, he responds nicely to verbal cues to keep his hands down. He tends to voice discontent through loud vocal sounds, which is also understandable due to his inability to verbalize his feelings. He is demonstrating a greater willingness to use his Canon communicator, typing such words as "stop," "over," "bathroom," "yes," and "no." At times the facilitator must "pull back" more when supporting Mark in his attempts at communication, possibly as a result of his frustration/agitation.

- As with all of us, Mark has good days and bad days. Conditions that may or may not affect other students such as establishing rapport, seating conditions, auditory and visual distractions, and/or medication may have a more profound effect on Mark's ability to demonstrate skills. Mark also appears to require ample "wait times." He responds well to consistency and clear, predictable expectations and can be quite affectionate and playful. Although the administration of the WJ-R was an attempt to obtain an idea of some of his skills, the results should be interpreted with some amount of caution due to the language based nature of this assessment tool.

This completed the basic preparations and testing that we judged prudent and as endorsed by Mr. Rugel.

CHAPTER 11

LEGAL MAPPING AND STRATEGIES
1994

A fter studying the dynamics of the circumstances facing us, Mr. Rugel wrote a trial planning memo that outlined our case from a legal perspective. In the memo, Mr. Rugel wrote:

Inclusion in the regular classroom is the presumptive placement for all disabled children under IDEA, 504, and the ADA.

A child may be removed from the regular classroom only if the school system can demonstrate that even with the use of auxiliary aids and services an appropriate educational program can not be implemented. The courts approach this analysis by asking the following questions:

1. Has the school made a reasonable effort to accommodate the child in the regular classroom?
2. What are the benefits available to the child in the regular classroom?
3. What are the negative side effects on the other students of the inclusion of the child in the regular classroom?

We will demonstrate that LCPS did not take appropriate steps to accommodate Mark. LCPS did not employ an inclusion coordinator, provide appropriate training to its staff, employ a reasonable behavior modification program, use facilitated communications to its best advantage, or modify the curriculum sufficiently.

While Mark may be participating to a great degree in "parallel instruction," we will establish that this is still more likely to benefit him than a shared curriculum in the self-contained model. And finally, we will show that Mark presents no danger to other students. At the very most, Mark's behavior may be distracting at times, but no more than the behavior of many other children whose behaviors are simply more familiar, i.e., hyperactivity, clowning, anger, etc.

Trial Planning/Witness List

The hearing had been set to begin August 15, 1994, and to continue on August 16th and August 30th, if necessary. Mr. Rugel had been given an August 8th deadline to submit our list of witnesses and exhibits. We developed the following list of supportive witnesses and outlined the purpose of testimony for each:

- Ms. Truax, principal, Butterfield School, was to describe the nature of the inclusion program in which Mark was successfully enrolled during kindergarten and first grade.
- Ms. Mrazek, teaching assistant, Butterfield School, was to describe how Mark was included and the nature of his success.
- Ms. Colley, inclusion facilitator in Montgomery County, was to review her observations of Mark in second grade, focus on the proposed IEP objectives, and discuss how those objectives could be implemented in the regular classroom. Ms. Colley was also prepared to critique the failed behavioral program that LCPS imposed on Mark and to compare it to a positive behavioral support plan that would work well with Mark.
- Ms. Ruppmann, our educational consultant who had formerly worked for LCPS and specifically on Mark's inclusion program, was to describe the ongoing process of working with LCPS. In particular, Ms. Ruppmann was prepared to provide an insider's view of Mr. Winters' actions to undermine Ms. Kelly's attempts to develop a successful inclusion program for Mark. She was to describe a meeting that Mr. Winters held with the Ashburn E.S. staff early in December, 1993. The purpose of Mr. Winters' meeting was to withdraw LCPS's support for Mark's inclusion program and to urge the staff to consider the Leesburg autism program as a more suitable placement for him.
- Ms. Thornton, the special education teacher who worked privately with Mark, was to provide evidence regarding Mark's academic abilities and to offer her positive opinion as to the likelihood of success in a regular classroom.

- We, as parents, were to describe the ongoing process of trying to develop an appropriate program for Mark at Ashburn E.S.

Pre-hearing Briefs

Mr. Rugel submitted a pre-hearing brief to the hearing officer, Ms. McBride, days before the start of the due process hearing. In that brief, Mr. Rugel pointed out to Ms. McBride that IDEA created a legal presumption establishing the right of all students to be educated in the regular classroom with their non-disabled peers, to the maximum extent appropriate. Further, section 504 of the Rehabilitation Act of 1973 revealed Congress' intent to protect children with handicaps from public school discrimination.

In his legal analysis, Mr. Rugel stated that LCPS was required to offer a "continuum of services" to educate children with disabilities in order to prohibit the exclusion of an entire category of children from the regular classroom based solely on their diagnosis or label. In effect, this meant that not only was the Loudoun County School Board required to make the continuum available, but it was also required to make individualized placement decisions for *each* child. Mr. Rugel commented that, all too often, IEPs and placement decisions were program-driven rather than student-driven, as they should be by law and by principle.

In order to remove Mark from the regular classroom, LCPS must show (1) that it offers a continuum of placements for children with autism, including a regular classroom with appropriate supplementary aides and services, and (2) that all alternatives are inappropriate using the tests outlined above. In addition, Mr. Rugel pointed out that IDEA does not require that a child be provided an education equal to that of a non-handicapped child. Therefore, any comparison of Mark's ability with the abilities of his classmates in the regular classroom was irrelevant. The issue was not how different Mark may look, act, or perform when compared to his classmates, but whether he would benefit from placement in the regular classroom.

LCPS presented its case in rather simple but compelling terms. Ms. Mehfoud, LCPS's attorney, basically alleged that the due process hearing resulted from LCPS's concerns that Mark's placement in a regular education classroom was inappropriate for his academic instruction. She proposed that evidence demonstrated that Mark did not derive educational benefit from academic instruction provided in a regular program.

Ms. Mehfoud described that although Mark is not able to talk, he can make sounds and, in fact, that he makes constant noise in class, crying and screeching. Additionally, Ms. Mehfoud characterized Mark as engaging in persistent misbehaviors in class. Those misbehaviors were identified as flapping his hands, throwing himself on the floor, laying down on the floor, kicking his feet, throwing temper tantrums, taking his shoes/clothes off, wandering around the class, hitting other students, pinching other students, filtering objects, and putting his hands down his pants to hold his penis.

Ms. Mehfoud also claimed that Mark's attention span was only two to three minutes, that he required frequent breaks, and that he was highly distractible.

LCPS's case rested upon several judgmental points that it proposed to establish as fact during the due process hearing:

- Mark does not model his peers. In fact he appears unaware of the presence of peers in the classroom.
- Mark functions at a pre-kindergarten level, making the disparity between Mark's educational functioning and that of his peers significant.
- Mark needs one-on-one instruction to learn, since his only academic gains have come when he was taught one-on-one.
- Mark's need for supplemental aides and services is too great for a regular class placement.
- Mark's placement in a regular classroom adversely affects students in his class.

Due Process Hearing – 1994

The first day of the due process hearing on August 15, 1994, was highly contentious from the start. The first issue to be addressed was whether or not Ms. McBride would allow television cameras into the hearing room. Ms. McBride was concerned about our preference to open the hearing to the public.

LCPS's position, per Ms. Mehfoud, was that the hearing should remain closed to protect the confidentiality of the child. On the other hand, we suspected that it simply was not in LCPS's best interest to allow their suit against us to be publicized. Not only would it question the school system's compliance with federal law, but it might also stir up a great deal of public sentiment. After consulting with the attorneys representing both sides of the issue and delaying the start of the hearing for more than an hour, Ms. McBride ultimately ruled that there would be no television cameras allowed in the hearing chambers. Nonetheless, she was compelled to open the hearing to the public, as we had requested.

The due process hearing was held over a five-day period (August 15, September 26 - 28, and October 27, 1994) during which twenty witnesses were called to give testimony. Local newspapers provided intense coverage of the hearing. After the story broke, an article focused on Mark and our legal case appeared in the October 17th edition of *People* magazine. We were also invited to appear on NBC's *Today Show* (October 17th) and on CBS's *This Morning* (October 26th). Ms. Mehfoud represented LCPS on the *Today Show* via a remote satellite connection. In addition, *Jim Lehre's News Hour* featured us in their investigative report on "Inclusive Education" on March 24, 1998.

While primarily focused on defending Mark's right to an inclusive education in Loudoun County, we also wanted to publicize the plight of all parents with disabled children who were trying to obtain a meaningful education for their children. In our view, too often these struggles are fought behind closed doors, and it was time to open the door to public scrutiny.

In the months that followed, we both appeared on television and radio talk shows throughout the United States. Our aim was to focus public attention on disabled children, special education, and inclusion, all the while talking about Mark and our own experiences with segregated special education programs vs. inclusion. As the legal process ensued, national newspapers (and even some foreign/international papers) kept track of our case and regularly printed updates. Additionally, Joseph appeared before a Congressional subcommittee to give testimony on our personal experiences with special education.

Post-hearing Briefs

Following the five-day hearing, in a 43-page memorandum written on behalf of Loudoun County Public Schools, Ms. Mehfoud outlined LCPS's legal position for the hearing officer, Ms. McBride. The introduction, as Ms. Mehfoud wrote it, provides the reader with justification for LCPS's position:

> Introduction: This hearing was initiated at the request of the Loudoun County Public Schools ("Loudoun") as a result of its concerns about the inappropriateness of the placement of Mark Hartmann ("Mark") in a regular education classroom for his academic instruction. There is no dispute between the parties about the fact that Mark should have some mainstreaming opportunities. Loudoun sincerely believes, however, that Mark will not and does not derive educational benefit from academic instruction provided in a regular program. Loudoun has proposed placing Mark in a class for autistic students to receive the academic portion of his instruction, while continuing to be mainstreamed in areas such as art, music, physical education, recess and library. This program provides the appropriate balance between his significant educational needs and

the opportunity for mainstreaming.

The decision made in this matter is critical because the decision affects Mark and other students who are presently educated in the class with Mark. Also, due to the lengthy nature of the administrative and judicial proceedings expected to follow this case, a final decision will not likely be made in time to change Mark's placement during the current school year. The determination made in this case will determine where Mark will be educated for the foreseeable future.

Mark is at a crossroads in his educational career. One road leads him to a classroom where he can learn the functional academic skills he needs and also learn to communicate. The other road continues him in a placement where he is maintained for alleged social reasons but where he cannot derive educational benefit. In the minds of the professionals from Loudoun the choice is a clear one. Mark's need to receive an appropriate education dictated the initiation of this hearing. Loudoun urges the hearing officer to order Mark's placement at Leesburg Elementary School so that Mark will receive the appropriate educational services to which he is entitled under the Individuals with Disabilities Education Act.

Our post-hearing brief, prepared by Mr. Rugel, focused on the deficiencies in Mark's inclusion program as implemented by LCPS at Ashburn E.S. Mr. Rugel summarized this by saying, "The school system failed to use appropriate supplemental aids and services which would permit Mark to benefit from an education in the regular classroom."

Mr. Rugel recounted the following facts highlighted by testimony during the hearing:

- No special education teacher was provided for Mark from September 1993 to the last week of February 1994.
- No member of Mark's educational team had significant experience working with children with autism.
- No permanent member of Mark's educational team had experience working with severely disabled children in an inclusion program.
- The school system failed to adequately train its personnel with respect to the process of inclusion or the nature of autism.
- The school system implemented no system to appropriately modify the curriculum for Mark.
- The school system failed to implement an appropriate behavior plan.

- The school system failed to provide appropriate related services.
- The school system failed to use public and private resources available to them to provide Mark with an appropriate educational program.

Mr. Rugel concluded his post hearing brief with a succinct summary of both sides of the case and encouraged the hearing officer to uphold our position:

> The school system comes before you requesting that it be permitted to change the placement of Mark Hartmann from a regular classroom to a self-contained classroom. In order to permit this change of placement you must find that Mark cannot derive an educational benefit from his present placement. It is clear that Mark can derive an educational benefit from his placement. It is equally clear that the lack of success of Mark's program at Ashburn E.S. lies on the school system's doorstep. The school system should not be permitted to change Mark's placement based on his lack of progress, when its own failures have caused this lack of progress. To permit the school system to unravel the intent of the IDEA in this manner would do a grave injustice to both Mark and the clear policies set out by the IDEA. On these grounds the school system's request must be denied.
>
> The hearing officer must also determine whether the program offered by the school system provides Mark with a free and appropriate public education. The facts establish that while Mark should remain in the regular classroom, he is also entitled to an appropriately implemented special education therein. The Hartmanns urge that the hearing officer make the following findings of fact and conclusions of law:
>
> 1. That Mark Hartmann can and must be educated in a regular classroom.
> 2. That the school system has failed to provide Mark Hartmann with a free and appropriate public education.
> 3. That the school system failed to provide Mark Hartmann with supplemental aids and services which would allow Mark to benefit from a special education in the regular classroom and to which he is entitled.

It is further requested that the school system be required to supplement Mark's special educational program by providing the services outlined by the Virginia Institute for Developmental Disabilities.

Now that the due process hearing was over and the post-hearing briefs were filed, we were left feeling absolutely disillusioned with public education. We simply could not rationalize the *betrayal of public trust* that we had witnessed, nor understand the extreme passive/aggressive behavior that LCPS educators had displayed in their dealings with us. At this juncture, we remained resolute in supporting Mark's right to an inclusive education. We'd witnessed the direct benefit of inclusive, supportive education during Mark's attendance at Butterfield School in Illinois. Now we were left to await the hearing officer's decision …

CHAPTER 12

McBRIDE'S DECISION
December 1994

It was Thursday afternoon, December 15, 1994, and Roxana had just returned home from shopping. She pressed the button on the answering machine to hear the messages waiting for her. One message was from a local newspaper reporter. He wanted to talk with us—to get our comment about the due process decision that had gone against us. Roxana sat motionless and in shock. To think that we would hear, like this! After collecting herself, she called Joseph at work and passed on the message. In turn, Joseph immediately called our attorney, Mr. Rugel. There was no answer. Joseph decided to leave work and to join Roxana at home.

Shortly after arriving home, Mr. Rugel called, stating that he had just received the decision from the hearing officer. Nonetheless, he told us that LCPS had announced the decision to the press at noontime, much earlier in the day. Mr. Edward Hamilton, superintendent of Loudoun County Public Schools, had given the following statement to the press concerning the decision:

> I am pleased that the hearing officer has affirmed the recommendations that have been made in this case by the professional staff at Loudoun County Public Schools. Since the beginning, this has been a case about one student's education, not about inclusion in general. We remain committed to providing appropriate educational opportunities to our disabled students in accordance with their needs, and will continue to make professional judgments on a case-by-case basis. I hope the Hartmanns will agree to proceed with the recommended IEP in accordance with the hearing officer's decision.

Ms. Mehfoud, LCPS's attorney, also made a statement to the press:

> Obviously, I'm very pleased that the school board's position in the hearing was vindicated. I hope the ruling will bring about an agreement between the Hartmanns and the school board on the best educational options for Mark.

Mr. Rugel informed us that the hearing officer, Ms. Nancy A. McBride, had written a twenty-six-page decision in favor of LCPS dated December 14, 1994. We listened silently as Mr. Rugel talked. At the end of the conversation, Joseph told Mr. Rugel that he would stop by his office to pick-up a copy of Ms. McBride's decision.

What had seemed so hopeful as we presented our case during five days of testimony was now shattered by the news. We were dismayed that Ms. McBride had given total credibility to the Ashburn E.S. teachers/staff and so little credibility to the witnesses that we brought in from Butterfield School. Further, Ms. McBride demonstrated a naïve, perhaps even juvenile depth of understanding regarding special education practices in the United States, which made it easy for LCPS to mislead her. We had hoped for a fair hearing, but instead witnessed yet another example of how stereotypes and preconceptions can influence a court's decision. We felt frustrated and defeated—and literally felt our confidence level slipping.

We asked Mr. Rugel to meet with the press on our behalf and to make a statement. Mr. Rugel gave a simple statement to the press: "They (the Hartmanns) are quite disappointed. They put their hearts and soul into this. They want the best for their child." Mr. Rugel also indicated that we would have no immediate comment on the ruling.

McBride's Decision

The following is a summary of Ms. McBride's decision from *Hartmann v. Loudon County Public Schools* (Due Process Hearing, 1994). Obvious rhetoric was omitted. Typographical errors as well as misspelled surnames appearing in Ms. McBride's decision are also corrected in the following abbreviated version (Author's note: We have included Ms. McBride's introductory remarks not to be duplicative, but to reveal the progression of her thinking as she rendered her decision). At the time of this decision, Mark had begun third grade in an inclusive setting at Ashburn E.S., pending the outcome of the hearing.

Introduction

The issue in this due process hearing is what is the appropriate program and placement for Mark Hartmann. The parents want Mark to remain in the regular education classroom of his neighborhood school with his non-disabled age peers. The school system initiated due process proceedings seeking to change Mark's placement to a self-contained autism class in a regular education school with mainstreaming for lunch, recess and non-academic subjects. The school system maintains that Mark cannot be educated satisfactorily in the regular classroom, even with the use of supplementary aids and services.

For reasons that are more fully set forth below, I find that the school system has established that Mark cannot be educated satisfactorily when he receives all, or almost all, of his instruction and related services in the regular classroom, even with the use of supplementary aids and services. I further find that the proposed placement in a self-contained autism class, located in a regular education school and providing opportunities for interaction with non-disabled peers is appropriate and constitutes the least restrictive environment.

Position of the parties

The School System

LCPS asserts that Mark Hartmann does not derive educational benefit from receiving education in the regular education classroom. Because of his disability, he requires instruction in a quiet, structured environment from professionals experienced in methods of special education. He has made no academic progress during his time of full inclusion. He also derives no significant benefit from being with his non-disabled peers. He does not initiate any interaction with them; he does not model their behavior, and in fact, seems indifferent to their presence. Mark's presence is very disruptive due to his constant vocalization, repeated screeching and screaming, and a host of other problem behaviors including crying, whining, kicking, pinching, biting, hitting, lying on the floor, removing his clothes and putting his hands inside his pants to hold his penis. In addition, Mark takes too much teacher time away from the other students. LCPS made every reasonable effort to include Mark and the conclusion is that he cannot be educated satisfactorily in a fully included setting. The proposed placement is appropriate for Mark. It affords him

Mark at 4 months

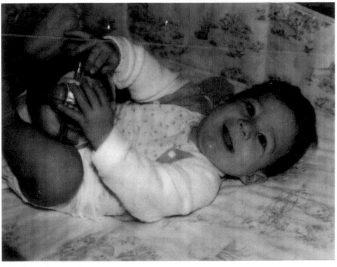

Mark at 5 months

*Mark at 4 years at Paces in
Newport News, Virginia*

Mark age 7 (portrait)

Mark, age 9, at Jerry Rugel's office

Mark, age 9, playing T-ball in Ashburn

Mark on field trip in 4th grade, Kipps E.S.

*Mark with 4th grade classmates at local pool,
age 11*

Mark in 3rd grade ready to go to the Kennedy Center, age 10

Mark 3rd grade at home in Ashburn

Mark with a school friend, Ami, age 14

The Hartmann Family; Mark age 9

Mark with 5th grade classmates during recess at Kipps E.S., age 12

Mark with 4th grade classmates at Kipps E.S. in auditorium, age 11

Mark with friends from school playing in the snow in Blacksburg, age 11

Mark and Laura playing in the snow with a friend in Ashburn, age 11

Mark, age 15, with Jamie Burke in Syracuse

Mark, age 13, celebrating Laura's birthday

Mark and Laura with friends at 8th grade dance

Mark, age 14, and Laura

Mark, age 14, with Laura at Christmas, 7th grade

Mark with Rosemary Crossley at Syracuse University Facilitated Communication Conference, age 14

Mark, age 14, with friends at home after school

Mark in 7th grade shopping at a local supermarket, age 14

Mark at home in Blacksburg, age 15

Mark, age 15, washing the family car

Mark with friends at home the night before Junior prom, age 17

Mark celebrating his 17th birthday with friends

Mark, age 17, getting haircut

Mark with his father after church, age 17

Mark age 18, carring Gatorade to football practice field

Mark age 18, working as the assistant manager for the Blacksburg High School football team, mixing Gatorade before summer time practice

Mark and David Hamrick at home after a long day at a conference, age 19

Mark after playing basketball, age 20

Junior Prom, age 17

Mark, age 17, enjoying dancing at junior prom with date

Senior year school picture, age 18

Mark, age 19, double dating for senior prom

Mark, age 19, graduation day with dad and Mr. Ferrell, Marks special education teacher during high school

Mark, age 19, graduation photo with Ms. Johanna Elliott, supervisor of special education at Blacksburg High School

*Mark, age 19, with Laura and Dad
on beach, Christmas 2006*

Mark getting ready to go to a wedding, age 19

Mark at Lucas McDuffy's wedding party, age 21

Mark and Laura at home in Blacksburg, age 22

Mark at the beach with his father, age 22

Mark, age 23, working at the sports medicine facility at VT

Mark, age 23, working at the sports medicine facility at VT

Mark, age 23, working at horticulture center at VT

Mark, age 23, working at Custom Catering Conference Center

placement in a group of five students with a trained special education teacher and aide, in a setting designed to suit his learning style and his sensory needs.

The Parents

The parents contend that Mark should receive all, or almost all, of his instruction and related therapies, within the regular education classroom. In their view, the law requires that Mark be educated in the regular classroom with such supplementary aids and services as will enable him to be educated satisfactorily. They believe that Mark has made progress in the included setting and that the unsatisfactory elements of Mark's performance relate to the failure of LCPS to implement properly his placement. If his curriculum is properly modified, he will not get frustrated and he will be able to make meaningful progress.

Mark exhibits certain non-typical behaviors that are related to his disability. Most of these behaviors are communicative. His vocalizations express his feelings, as do his frustrated, aggressive behaviors such as hitting or kicking. While these behaviors might seem random and meaningless, they have meaning for Mark and a proper behavior management program would discern that meaning and devise an appropriate strategy to minimize or eliminate the behavior. Some of the behaviors are not misbehaviors.

As is typical of persons with autism, Mark is impaired in his social relationships. Although he does not typically initiate interaction, he does model and interact with other children. Through his placement in the regular classroom, he has learned some social skills.

Mark's education at Ashburn has not been satisfactory because the staff has not implemented it properly. The staff had no expertise or experience in inclusion or autism. They were not provided the necessary supports or training to enable them to work with Mark in a successful way. Mark was not given the supplementary aids and services necessary for his success. LCPS did not make reasonable efforts to accommodate him in the regular classroom. The teacher and aide were untrained in inclusion and in autism. They were not given the necessary assistance in modifying the curriculum for Mark. They did not develop a behavior management plan. All of Mark's behaviors are communicative.

The included setting provides significant and proven benefits for Mark. He has benefited from the interaction with his non-disabled peers. He has learned to model their behavior in such matters as following the daily routine and hanging up his backpack. He has also grown in his ability to interact with others, especially with his peers.

The segregated setting, on the other hand, offers unknown and unproven results. Mark cannot learn appropriate social and communication skills in a program where his only peers are four children with autism, each of whom has serious communication impairments of his or her own. The mainstreaming opportunities provided in the proposed program are unstructured and will not provide a meaningful opportunity for social interaction and peer modeling.

The negative effect on other children has been distorted by the school system. The other children learned to tune out Mark's noises and continue with their work. Mark has a positive effect on the other children, teaching them to accept differences. If the classroom teacher spent too much time on Mark, it is because she was not adequately supported. An inclusion specialist should complete the curriculum modifications required for Mark.

The appropriate program for Mark is full inclusion in the regular education third grade classroom at the neighborhood school. Although this does not mean that every minute of his program must be delivered in the regular class, it is expected that the vast majority of it in fact would be in the regular class.

Findings of Fact

• Mark is a nine-year old child with a disability who requires special education and related services for him to benefit from his education.

• Autism is a complex disorder associated with varying levels of impairment.

• Mark was first identified as a child with a disability and found eligible for special education in March 1988. He has been receiving special education services since that time.

• Mark is very affected by many of the impairments typically associated with autism. He has no oral speech and he lacks a consistent communication system for identifying his needs and wishes for others. His receptive language is considerably stronger; he understands and responds to many commands and other communications.

• Mark's cognitive functioning is quite depressed, but his true ability in this area is not known. Due to his disability, he is not testable under standard conditions. Even when test instruments are adapted for him, the results yielded do not necessarily reflect his ability. The school system's assertion that Mark is mentally retarded was not established. Until Mark succeeds in expanding his expressive language skills, any opinion about Mark's cognitive ability is speculative. His reported competence in certain technical tasks and testing reports submitted by the parents indicate that he should be viewed as being in the average range for cognitive ability until a more definitive determination can be made.

•Mark is very impaired in his social interactions. At least outside of the home setting, Mark does not initiate social interaction.

•Because of sensory system irregularities, Mark seeks tactile stimulation through such activities as rubbing elbows of people working with him, filtering small objects, such as rice, beans and mulch through his fingers, and tossing and stroking objects such as stuffed animals.

•Ashburn principal Lynn Meadows testified that the class to which Mark was assigned was reduced from 26 to 21 and it was composed of second graders who tended to be more independent and higher functioning than other second graders. Ms. Debra Jarrett, the second grade teacher, was chosen for Mark because of her excellent teaching abilities. A full-time one-on-one aide was hired for Mark. He received 5 hours per week of speech and language therapy from Ms. Cristina Conroy-Winters. Jarrett, Conroy-Winters, and the aide worked closely together to coordinate and share information regarding Mark's placement. Ms. Jarrett and the aide received training in facilitated communication, a communication system that Mark had been using in Illinois. Ms. Conroy-Winters was familiar with facilitated communication and obtained advanced training through a consultation with an outside expert in the use of this model.

•The efforts of the Ashburn E.S. staff were under the supervision of the director of special education, Ms. Meagan Kelly. Ms. Kelly has extensive training in inclusion, having participated in an inclusion project, known as the Virginia Systems Change Project. She provided an in-service training on inclusion for the staff at Ashburn E.S. In October 1993, she also arranged for Mark's team, Ms. Meadows, Ms. Jarrett, the aide, and Ms. Conroy-Winters, to attend a full-day off-site workshop on inclusion. During the fall, LCPS personnel working with Mark also obtained consultations from educational consultants Jamie Ruppmann and Gail Mayfield. Mr. Fred Jernigan, the special education supervisor of the county's programs for autistic children, was also involved, especially with questions about managing Mark's behaviors. The curriculum for Mark was continually adapted or modified until his level of functioning was identified.

•The parents argue that at some point LCPS began to withdraw support. I do not find this to be the case. It should be noted that, rather than withdrawing for Mark's placement at Ashburn, the team recommended that it be continued at the time of the Ashburn IEP in March 1994. I infer no lack of commitment from an ongoing consideration of the success of Mark's programming.

•Mark's reading skills are at a pre-kindergarten level.

•In math, Mark understands counting. He can fill in missing numbers on a number line that goes up to 100. He cannot add with symbols, i.e., "2 + 3 = 5," but he can derive sums less than ten by counting two sets of objects on a number line.

•Mark learns best in a 1:1 setting. He is easily distracted by noise and visual stimulation. Mark has a relatively short attention span and needs frequent breaks. Mark learns by repetition and by practice. He requires a lot of structure and is disturbed by unanticipated changes.

•Mark exhibits many behaviors associated with autism, many of which are deemed undesirable. These behaviors are inappropriate in a regular classroom setting. Mark is a big strong child who cannot be easily restrained when he engages in injurious behaviors such as hitting, kicking, pinching and biting. Mark hits and pinches others several times a day. He is most likely to exhibit these behaviors when he is frustrated by material that is new or difficult or which he does not want to do.

•Mark requires a disproportionate amount of the time of the regular classroom teacher. Ms. Jarrett testified that some children who needed extra time in Mark's class last year did not get what they needed because Mark got any extra time that she had.

•Mark does not exhibit awareness of or interest in his peers in school. He does not initiate communication or any form of interaction with them. He does not model their behavior. He performs classroom routines from memory and with the assistance of verbal reminders. He will return a high-five greeting to a classmate. Mark has learned to comply with many of the routines and behaviors required in the regular education classroom.

•Socially, Mark remained quite isolated. His peers were fond of Mark, interested in him, eager to participate in classroom activities with him, and protective of him. Mark did not initiate social interaction with his peers. Despite teaching and prompting, he is unable to identify any of his classmates by name.

•Mark was not able to work on any of the same skills that second graders worked on last year and the same is true with respect to his third grade classmates this year. Mark was placed in a small reading group, but did not read along with the group. He was not able to answer comprehension questions when a story at the Grade 1.6 reading level was read aloud to him.

•Mark made no measurable academic progress attributable to his placement in the regular classroom. He did not participate in the regular curriculum, but was provided his own curriculum.

•Mark made great strides in learning to express himself on the communication board, devised by Cristina Conroy-Winters. In that time, Mark began to use the board to communicate spontaneously with adults and he was able to express three- or four-word sentences on the board.

•Mark made progress when he worked with a private tutor. The tutor, Ms. Cathy Thornton, is a certified special education teacher with five years of current experience as a teacher of autistic children. She was retained by the Hartmanns to tutor Mark and to attempt to measure his level of functioning. She found Mark's attention span, when working in a comfortable, one-on-one setting to be much greater than that displayed in the classroom. Based on her work with Mark, she believes that he is not mentally retarded.

•Mark learns best with one-to-one instruction, in a setting with minimal distractions. He needs to be learning skills that will help him to live an independent life in the future. His primary educational need at this time is the acquisition of a communication system, by which he can express preferences and needs.

•The school system demonstrated an intense and unexplained interest in Mark's eating habits. Its concern appears to have originated with the parent's decision to remove Mark from school during the lunch period and take him home for lunch. Its suspicions were fueled by the fact that Mark would return to school in the afternoon wearing a clean shirt, creating an apparent belief that his eating was so messy that he had to change his clothes. I remain at a loss as to why there were so many questions regarding Mark's eating habits and preferences. For that matter, compared to Mark's other needs, daily living skills such as self-feeding and dressing do not appear to be priorities for Mark.

•It cannot be determined how much progress Mark is capable of achieving. The answer to this question hinges on the acquisition by

Mark of a system for communication.

•Socially, Mark made some gains during the past year. He learned to tap a person's elbow lightly to get his or her attention. He learned to make certain wishes known through the use of his communication board.

Analysis

The case presents two issues: 1) whether the proposal to remove Mark from the regular classroom violates the obligation of LCPS to educate him, to the maximum extent appropriate, with non-disabled children; and 2) whether the proposed placement is appropriate for Mark.

Under the Individuals with Disabilities Education Act (IDEA), a child with a disability is entitled to a free and appropriate public education. An appropriate education is one that is tailored to the unique needs and abilities of the individual child and is reasonably calculated to enable the child to receive educational benefits. This was held in Board of Education v. Rowley (1982).

The point is clear from the language of the statute that there is a strong presumption in favor of education for children with disabilities in the regular education environment, alongside children who are not disabled. This requirement has been known as mainstreaming. The term "inclusion" is increasingly used to capture the essence of this requirement. Neither term appears in IDEA. For many individuals involved in education, the two terms bespeak certain philosophical or political differences as well as differing assumptions and values. The philosophical debate embodied by the use of these two terms is not susceptible to resolution in a legal proceeding. These words are sometimes viewed as terms that have been adopted to discuss delivery of the IDEA requirement to provide special education and related services in the least restrictive environment. They are used in the following discussion to denote points on a continuum of educational services.

I. Does the proposal of LCPS to remove Mark from the regular classroom violate its obligation to educate him, to the maximum extent approprite, with non-disabled children?

Courts have articulated slightly different standards to resolve the tension between the requirement for education in the mainstream with the requirement for specially designed education tailored to the unique needs and abilities of the child with a disability. In order to determine whether a school district is in compliance with IDEA's mainstreaming requirement, three circuits (5th Cir. 1989; 3rd Cir. 1993; 9th Cir. 1994) have adopted a two-part test first articulated in the case of Daniel R.R. v. State Board of Education. This test has not been accepted or rejected by the Fourth Circuit and it provides a logical framework for analyzing the problem.

A) Whether the child can be educated satisfactorily in a regular classroom with supplementary aids and services.

In considering the first part of this test, the courts consider several factors. They look at the steps that the school had taken to try to include the child in a regular classroom, a comparison between the educational benefits of the regular classroom environment, and, in some cases, the cost of inclusion. Applying this analysis to the question of the appropriate education for Mark Hartmann, I find that education in the regular classroom with the use of supplementary aids and services cannot be achieved satisfactorily.

i) Reasonable effort to accommodate.

In reaching this conclusion, I consider first whether reasonable efforts have been made to accommodate Mark in the regular classroom and I find that the efforts of this school system in this regard were reasonable. "The Act does not permit states to make mere token gestures to accommodate handicapped students; its requirement for modifying and supplementing regular education is broad." Daniel R.R., at 1048. Loudoun County undertook a serious effort to make full inclusion work for Mark. The principal placed Mark with a capable and willing teacher, and made modifications to the size and composition of the class. Ms. Jarrett prepared the other students for Mark and succeeded in creating a peer environment of support and affection for Mark. She gave Mark extra instructional time and modified and adapted the second grade curriculum to address his needs and find an instructional level and style that was appropriate for him. A full-time instructional aide was hired to work exclusively with Mark.

Meagan Kelly, the director of special education provided inservice training on inclusion, with reference to autism, to the personnel at Ashburn Elementary. Both Ms. Jarrett and the aide were trained in facilitated communication, an augmentative communication system that Mark had been using in Illinois. In October, Ms. Kelly also insured that she and the members of Mark's team—i.e., the classroom teacher, the aid, the speech and language teacher, the principal, and the special education supervisor of the autism program--attended a full-day workshop on inclusion.

Mark received five hours a week of speech and language therapy from Ms. Cristina Conroy-Winters. The group that worked with Mark identified as a team and worked diligently to formulate strategies that would enhance Mark's education. Although Mark's Illinois IEP did not provide for any special education services, LCPS added this component in February to provide more support for his education.

The parents contend that the school system failed to develop a behavior management plan to address Mark's troubling behaviors and that proper support in this area is crucial to mainstreaming or including a child like Mark. The record shows that, as early as October, Mark's challenging behaviors were identified as a potential problem. Fred Jernigan was consulted at that time for assistance and the team was involved in devising ways to manage Mark's behavior. In February, Fred Jernigan was added as a regular team member to meet weekly on issues of behavior. Although the parents have advocated for specific behavior management strategies, the school system was not required to adopt any particular methodology.

In view of the fact that the school system provided training for the regular education personnel, hired a full-time aide, addressed behavior management issues, modified and adapted the curriculum, and increased services when the need became apparent, I conclude that the school system's efforts to provide supplementary aides and services were sufficient.

ii) Compare educational benefits of regular classroom with education benefits of segregated classroom.

The second factor to consider in determining whether Mark can be educated satisfactorily in the regular classroom is a comparison of the benefits of regular education with those of special education. Mark has not demonstrated the receipt of any educational benefit from education in an included setting. The only gains made by Mark were his progress on the communication board in speech and language with Ms. Conroy-Winters and in his tutoring sessions with Cathy Thornton. It is clear that Mark learns best, and perhaps only, when a special education teacher in a 1:1 setting is teaching him. Because it appears that Mark is, in fact, capable of academic progress (in which I include communication skills), the comparison of educational benefit is a very important part of this analysis.

Mark's curricular goals are totally different from those of regular education students of his age. During class time, he was working on things that were totally different. He did not learn anything with the large group or in a small reading group or cooperative learning group.

Mark did learn to follow certain classroom routines and to stay seated during group activities that did not place any demands upon him. However, his language needs are too pervasive for him to acquire any meaningful benefit in this area simply from being educated alongside non-disabled peers. The limited benefits that Mark has received from his experience in the regular classroom demonstrate the continued need for meaningful contact with non-disabled peers. The fact that he has received virtually no educational benefit in the included setting weighs heavily in the determination that he cannot be educated satisfactorily in the regular education classroom. Moreover, the limited social benefits received in the regular setting are fully available in the mainstreaming proposed for Mark at Leesburg Elementary School.

iii) Effect of inclusion on the teacher and on other children.

The efforts of LCPS in providing supplementary aides and services to accommodate Mark has been fully discussed and deemed to be sufficient. In spite of those efforts, Mark engages in very disruptive behavior. Accepting the view that these behaviors are communicative and are a direct result of Mark's disability, they are, nevertheless, disruptive and have a negative effect on the environment in the classroom.

Considered alone, the negative effects of Mark's placement in the regular classroom might not be enough to justify removing him from the regular classroom, but they do come into the balance as a negative. Mark's vocalizations are continual throughout the day. Witnesses testified that last year he was kicking, biting, or hitting approximately three times a day. Although the children apparently learned to tune out some of this behavior, the daily disturbances do result in down time while the children are distracted and then redirected. Mark also presents some physical safety concerns. He is physically aggressive, involved in kicking, biting, pinching, and hitting. It is not contended that Mark is mean or otherwise possessed of bad intent when he engages in these behaviors. But the result is the same for the classmate or the teacher who is the recipient of these behaviors. He has tended to strike out at his teachers, who while slightly better able to protect themselves from his attacks, are reasonable in perceiving some physical danger. Finally, Mark's full-time presence in the classroom demands a disproportionate amount of the planning and classroom time of the regular teacher.

To be sure, there are positive effects to having Mark in the classroom. Non-disabled children learn to accept and accommodate differences among people. This desirable effect certainly occurred in second grade. Ms. Jarrett reported that the other students were fond of Mark and eager to be his partner. She stated that they were very protective of him.

Although I find Mark's presence in the classroom to be disruptive and the threat of his aggressive physical behaviors to be significant and daily, I do not believe that this factor, considered alone, would necessarily warrant excluding him from the regular education classroom. The negative effects of Mark's full-time inclusion in the regular education setting, considered with the efforts of the school system to provide supplementary aids and services and the absence of educational benefit to him from the setting, however, further support the conclusion that Mark cannot be educated satisfactorily in the regular classroom.

B. Whether the proposed program includes the child to the maximum extent appropriate.

The program proposed by LCPS provides for mainstreaming in all non-academic activities: act, music, physical education, library, and recess. This gives Mark a significant opportunity to interact with non-disabled peers on a regular and daily basis, while receiving his academic instruction and related services in a manner from which he will derive educational benefit.

II. Is the proposed placement appropriate?

A separate question posed, and one that must always be answered in any due process proceeding, is whether the proposed placement is appropriate. A placement is appropriate if it is reasonably calculated to provide educational benefit. I find that the self-contained autism class at Leesburg, with mainstreaming for art, music, library, physical education, and recess, is reasonably calculated to provide educational benefit for Mark.

The parents contend that the self-contained program is not appropriate because its benefits, if any, are unproven. The proponent of a program or placement does not bear a burden of proving that it will be effective; rather, it must be proven that the proposed program or placement is reasonably calculated to provide educational benefit. The proposed placement offers a structured program with a ratio of 5 students (including Mark) to one special education teacher and an aide. The classroom has instructional materials suited to Mark's learning style and offers break activities, such as a swing, that will satisfy his sensory needs.

The parents have expressed concern about the value of the proposed mainstreaming. Through their witnesses, they have highlighted the challenges of mainstreaming in the relatively unstructured environments of recess and the so-called "specials"--music, art, library and physical education. Mindful of these concerns, I direct that the IEP reflect objectives for Mark related to his mainstream participation. In furtherance of this, I also direct that the IEP reflect a requirement that Mark is always accompanied by a teacher or an aide in the mainstream environment until such time as he can demonstrate an ability to be there independently. I also direct that the IEP reflect that he have his specials with the same regular education class. Mark has tremendous difficulty in adjusting to change. Furthermore, he cannot hope to have meaningful social contact if he is moving through different groups of 25 students.

The school system must, of course, adapt the autism program to suit Mark's unique needs and abilities. It is Mark's IEP that must be implemented in this setting, not just that of a "typical" autistic child. The needs addressed must be his needs, not needs presumed to exist because he is autistic. The benefit of the setting for Mark is the opportunity to have his goals addressed through specialized instruction from trained educational professionals in a structured setting, with a small student teacher ratio. As reflected in Mark's IEP, his goals and objectives relate to the following areas; the acquisition of a means of communication and the development of language; improved interpersonal skills and replacement of inappropriate behaviors; academic growth in math and reading. Daily living skills are not part of his IEP and it is expected that they would be only an incidental part of his program under that IEP.

The parents also assert that the IEP committee was not free to act independently because of pressure brought to bear on its members by Mr. NeilWinters, LCPS Director of Pupil Services. This contention is based on a belief that Mr. Winters expressed negative opinions about Mark's placement at Ashburn to various team members, all of who were his subordinates. The only direct evidence of this was the testimony of Jamie Ruppmann regarding remarks made by Mr. Winters at a December 1993 team meeting. The fact that Mr. Winters is married to Ms. Conroy-Winters, the speech and language pathologist is also advanced as evidence of pressure and an improper predetermination of placement. Regardless of Mr. Winters' opinions and regardless of whether he expressed them to individuals responsible for making a placement decision on Mark, I do not find that he put pressure on the team. Each member of the team testified as to his or her own professional opinion as to what was best for Mark. Moreover, an IEP issued in March 1994, three months after the alleged pressure, recommended continued inclusion at Ashburn, further negating any inference of undue pressure.

Conclusion

For the reasons stated above, I find that the proposed placement is appropriate and that it satisfies the IDEA requirement for education in the least restrictive environment. I direct that the IEP be modified to address goals and support for the mainstreaming components of Mark's placement.

   ~ Hearing officer

CHAPTER 13

NEW BEGINNINGS
Holidays 1994

Trying to sideline our emotions over Ms. McBride's decision, our family concentrated on making Christmas 1994 as memorable as possible for Mark and Laura. Roxana's sister and brother-in-law, Aida and Alvin, and their three children (ages 12, 8 and 5) joined us for the holidays. Joseph's carpool buddy, Chris, agreed to play Santa Claus on Christmas Eve to give the children a special treat. We rented the Santa suit and took Roxana and Aida over to talk with Chris about each child so that he would know just the right thing to say to each of them, individually.

Late Christmas Eve, as both of our families watched TV in the family room, Santa arrived, shaking sleigh bells as he approached the front door of the house. He entered unannounced and began bringing all of the children's toys into the house. The twenty-four-inch bicycle for Laura came in first, followed by large bags of toys that Santa dutifully emptied, carefully placing each gift around our Christmas tree. Christina (the youngest, at 5 years old) was the first to hear the sleigh bells—she alerted the other children. They all went into the dining room to "see what the matter was." Discovering Santa busy at work, the children remained silent and hid under the dining room table and behind walls, soaking up the performance. At just the right moment, Santa took note of the children and called out to each of them by name. One-by-one, he asked each of them to come forward. Santa spoke to each child, including Mark, about the past year and what each had to do to remain on his "nice list." After his little talk, Santa gave each child a large candy cane as his special gift.

Chris had memorized all the key points the mothers had given him about each child; he was perfect in his recall. Roxana, Aida, Alvin and Joseph watched as the children were mesmerized by Santa's insightful words. With a "Ho, Ho, Ho" and a "Merry Christmas," Santa left the house and disappeared into the night. The children were flabbergasted!

When the children realized that Santa had delivered a two-wheeled bicycle for Laura, their imaginations caught fire. Since they had not seen Santa bring the bicycle into the house, they were *convinced* that he had brought in miniature-sized toys that grew to full size after he placed them under the Christmas tree! For that moment, we all experienced one of those cherished events that will live on forever in the hearts of our children.

Answering the Question ... What's next?

During a December 16th meeting at his office in Herndon, Virginia, Mr. Rugel told us that an appeal of the due process decision could drag on for a year or more. Further, he said that with the stay-put provision of IDEA, Mark would remain in an included placement at Ashburn E.S. until the legal process was concluded. Nonetheless, we were both leery. We judged that it was not in LCPS's best interest to work toward building a successful inclusion program for Mark while the legal process continued. Therefore, instead of continuing a basically unsatisfactory placement in third grade, we decided to remove Mark from Ashburn E.S., altogether.

Mark's last day at Ashburn Elementary School was the day before Christmas Break began in late December, 1994. While this was a scary step, it was one of the best decisions we ever made.

As for options, we could abide by Ms. McBride's ruling and change Mark's placement to the self-contained autism class in Leesburg, but this option was flat out unacceptable to us. Mr. Rugel mentioned the principal at Sterling E.S. who was respected by parents of children involved in a mainstreaming program at his school. Thus, the second option was to talk with this principal about developing a unique program suited to Mark that would also be acceptable to LCPS. While Mark would not be fully included at Sterling E.S., it could be the next best option. The third possibility was to develop a home-bound program for Mark wherein LCPS would provide all required services at home, similar to the work that Ms. Thornton had done with Mark. After giving the idea some thought, we concluded that coordinating with LCPS to that degree would be too difficult and emotionally taxing.

Still trying to brainstorm other viable options, Roxana remembered Butterfield School and how supportive Ms. Sandy Truax had been. She wondered if we could move back to Lombard, Illinois and enroll Mark into the second half of third grade at Butterfield School. Focusing only on the positive aspects of this option, we especially liked this idea.

Then Roxana suggested that we should call Ms. Kenna Colley, the inclusion specialist in Blacksburg, Virginia. Ms. Colley knew the educational ropes in Virginia and could possibly recommend a placement for Mark outside of Loudoun County. In fleshing out that idea, we reasoned that Mark could attend the school where Ms. Colley now taught—Kipps Elementary School in Blacksburg, Virginia. We reached for the roadmap of Virginia. Blacksburg was located in Montgomery County, approximately 250 miles west of Ashburn. This was an idea worth investigating since we knew that the schools in Montgomery County looked upon inclusion favorably for children with disabilities.

As such, we decided to visit Blacksburg during the Christmas holiday to assess the possibility of relocating there. We arrived in Blacksburg on December 31st for our New Year's Eve celebration at a hotel just outside of town. Laura and Mark enjoyed the travel adventure.

The next day, we drove around Blacksburg, found Kipps E.S., and checked on the availability/cost of apartment rentals close to the school. We were impressed with Blacksburg as a relatively small university town (home to Virginia Tech). If LCPS would not agree to Sterling E.S. as an alternative placement for Mark in Loudoun County, then we were prepared to relocate Mark to Blacksburg, Virginia—in Montgomery County and another school system entirely.

Thus, early in 1995, we contacted the principal at Sterling E.S. and set up a meeting to discuss appropriate programs for Mark as an alternative to the autism program in Leesburg. While the principal may have been willing to work things out with us, LCPS was not.

In addition, while we were still weighing the advisability of appealing Ms. McBride's decision, Mr. Rugel informed us that Ms. Mehfoud had mentioned in conversation that *LCPS was considering filing an injunction that would prevent Mark from attending his neighborhood school during the appeal process.* This would effectively negate the stay-put provision of the law held in force during the due process proceedings. This compelling factor helped prompt our decision: Roxana and Mark would re-locate to Blacksburg.

On January 3, 1995, Mr. Rugel filed an administrative appeal of Ms. McBride's due process decision on our behalf through the Office of Special Programs, Division of Compliance, within the Virginia Department of Education. The Supreme Court of Virginia subsequently appointed Mr. Alexander N. Simon to serve as the administrative appeals officer, giving him 45 days to review the case and make his decision.

In a letter dated January 17, 1995, we notified family and friends of the issues we were facing. In the letter, Roxana explained the ruling of the due-process hearing and our decision to appeal that ruling. Additionally, we told of our decision to enroll Mark at Kipps Elementary School in Blacksburg, even though it was more than 250 miles from our home. We shared our hope that the second half of third grade in a properly run inclusion program would again establish that Mark *could benefit* from being fully included in school alongside his peers, if the program was done right.

Laura and Joseph would continue to reside in Ashburn. Roxana and Mark would now reside in Blacksburg.

CHAPTER 14

INJUSTICE – MONTGOMERY COUNTY PUBLIC SCHOOLS
1995

After signing a contract on a one-bedroom apartment in Blacksburg, Virginia, Roxana registered Mark in school. Mr. Ray E. Van Dyke, the principal at Kipps Elementary School, was required by regulation to make a temporary placement decision regarding Mark. On January 20, 1995, Mr. Van Dyke talked with Ms. Meadows at Ashburn E.S. to obtain enough information about Mark's program to make a decision. The details of Mark's IEP were discussed, and Mr. Van Dyke decided to temporarily place Mark in a fully inclusive third-grade setting with appropriate supports and accommodations. The record of his conversation with Ms. Meadows, included with his decision on placement, was faxed to the director of Special Education for Montgomery County Public Schools (MCPS) on January 24th, for her information and as a matter of courtesy.

On January 21st, Roxana and Mark moved into their new home at Fox Ridge Apartments to begin their six-month lease. Located in the college town of Blacksburg, Fox Ridge preferred to have all leases expire in June, at the end of the school year, rather than at odd times during the year (which could result in months of no occupancy). We were lucky to have found a vacant apartment, especially one within walking distance of Kipps E.S. Roxana immediately began finding out all that was required for residency. Within a week, she had changed her driver's license, registered her car, and taken other less formal steps to establish her residency in Blacksburg/Montgomery County.

At Kipps E.S., Mr. Van Dyke selected a third-grade teacher to work with Ms. Colley to develop Mark's IEP. He also began the process of identifying a teacher's assistant to support Mark and another special education student in their fully inclusive placements. Mr. Van Dyke set January 26th for the IEP meeting and Friday, January 27th, as the date that Mark would begin school.

Roxana agreed that having Mark begin on a Friday was a perfect plan to introduce him to the new school. Nonetheless, it was not to be.

Collusion ... and Another Obstacle

Unbeknownst to us, sometime during the week of January 23rd, LCPS contacted Mr. Herman G. Bartlett, Jr., Superintendent of Schools for Montgomery County. While the nature of LCPS's discussions with Mr. Bartlett, Jr. is not known, subsequent actions speak loud and clear.

Early on the morning of January 26th, the day that she was to sign Mark's IEP at Kipps E.S., Roxana received a knock at her apartment door. There stood Ms. Patricia M. Radcliffe, Director of Special Education for Montgomery County Public Schools, and Mr. Van Dyke, Kipps E.S. principal. Ms. Radcliffe hand-delivered the following message to Roxana from Mr. Bartlett, Jr., in a letter dated January 26, 1995:

> As the superintendent of the Montgomery County Public School System, I am charged with supervising the schools in Montgomery County. I am sure that you are aware that the public school system is required to make available a free public education to those students who reside within Montgomery County.
>
> Montgomery County Public Schools (MCPS) staff members have received information which causes me to question whether you are entitled to enroll Mark in the MCPS. The MCPS system will provide an education to Mark if he is a resident of Montgomery County. However, that threshold question must first be addressed.
>
> In order to assist the school system in determining whether you are a legal resident of Montgomery County, please complete the enclosed questionnaire. Your response should be sworn in the presence of a notary. In addition, the School Division will be happy to consider any other information that you provide.
>
> We are in hopes of resolving the issue of residence as soon as possible. Thank you for your prompt response to the enclosed questionnaire.
>
> ~ Sincerely, Herman G. Bartlett, Jr.

The questionnaire accompanying the letter listed the following questions:

1. Are you involved in administrative litigation which is pending currently relating to Mark's placement in another school

system? If so, which locality?

What is the current status of any pending administrative litigation?

2. Does your family live in Loudoun County?
3. Does Mark have other siblings enrolled in school in other localities?
4. Do you own a residence in another locality?
   If so, which locality?
5. Do you own a residence in Montgomery County?
6. Do you own any motor vehicles?
   If so, what is the address of the registration?
   If that address was changed recently, give the date of the change.
7. Do you have a valid driver's license?
   What address is registered with the Department of Motor Vehicles for that driver's license?
   If that address was changed recently, give the date of the change.
8. Please provide your current address, if any, in Montgomery County.
   Do you have a lease?
   If so, on what date did you execute the lease?
   What is the term of the lease?
   Describe the premises that are the subject of the lease. (House or apartment? Number of bedrooms, baths?)
9. Are you registered to vote?
   If so, in what state and locality are you registered?
10. Please provide any additional information which will assist the Montgomery County Public Schools in determining whether you are a legal resident.

Ms. Radcliffe told Roxana that Mark's registration and attendance at Kipps E.S. could not go forward until Roxana and Mark established that they were residents of Montgomery County.

Later, it would come to light that Ms. Radcliffe made this personal visit to Roxana's new apartment to see the actual quantity and quality of furnishings, therein. Ms. Radcliffe was required to gain this personal observation so that she could testify in court against us regarding the issue of residency. It is clear that Ms. Radcliffe was not acting out of her own volition, but rather simply following instructions from MCPS administrators. Roxana, already emotionally frayed from Ms. McBride's due process decision favoring LCPS, was distraught. She called Joseph at work. He could tell that she was on the brink of an emotional breakdown.

Roxana and Mark returned to Ashburn for the weekend. We prepared answers to the questionnaire and wrote a personal letter to Mr. Bartlett, Jr. that outlined our circumstances in detail. The letter also stated our firm intention that Roxana and Mark would continue to reside in Montgomery County for the foreseeable future. We sent the letter and completed questionnaire to the MCPS central office in Christiansburg, Virginia by Federal Express. The package arrived on Monday morning, January 30th.

A Second Lawsuit

Without waiting for our response, however, MCPS had already filed a bill of complaint in the circuit court of Montgomery County against us! The bill of complaint, dated January 27th, alleged that Mark was not entitled to enrollment in the public schools of Montgomery County because he was not a resident of the county. Further, MCPS requested that the court enter into force a temporary injunction prohibiting Roxana and/or Joseph from attempting to enroll Mark in the public schools of the county until the court ruled on the merits of the declaratory judgment. Our letter to Mr. Bartlett, Jr. and response to the questionnaire would be used by MCPS *against us* in a court trial over the issue of residency. Montgomery County Circuit Court Judge Ray Grubbs set February 16th as the trial date to hear arguments. We now faced a *second lawsuit!*

Mr. Rugel judged that the lawsuit brought against us by MCPS bordered on harassment. After all, how many families in Virginia are routinely subjected to the stress of completing a questionnaire obviously prepared by legal counsel on behalf of the school district, prior to registering their children for school? Mr. Rugel concluded that the only recourse was to present a defense in court that would demonstrate, unequivocally, that Roxana and Mark were legitimate residents of Montgomery County, Virginia.

Mr. Rugel said that due to the residency requirement of the law alone, Montgomery County was obligated to provide a free and appropriate public education for Mark. He told us that the only time a school system is free not to enroll a child is when that child is living with someone other than the natural parent for the sole purpose of education, such as a child living with an aunt or an uncle. This simply was not our case. We were encouraged by Mr. Rugel's positive assessment of these new legal issues being thrown at us.

The press in both Montgomery County and in Loudoun County carried the news of this second lawsuit filed by a Virginia school district against us over Mark's education. Ms. Jamie Ruppmann, the educational consultant for

LCPS who had now become our close ally and personal friend, prepared a statement on our behalf. This statement was delivered to members of the Virginia General Assembly, in Richmond, on February 8th. In the final paragraph, Ms. Ruppmann wrote:

> Are all Virginia's children and families treated in this manner? Given that the planning in Montgomery County Public Schools for Mark's enrollment was well under way, why did school officials suddenly take such a serious action against this child? Is there ever going to be a point where enough is enough? Virginia's children and youth with disabilities are deeply loved and valued by their families. We cannot and will not stand by in silence while public school officials in the Commonwealth pursue these coercive and discriminatory actions.

Subsequently, on February 13th, Ms. Ruppmann's statement was released to the press and endorsed by:
- Parents of Down Syndrome Children of Northern Virginia
- The Association of Severely Handicapped Children of Northern Virginia
- The Autism National Committee
- The Parent Educational Advocacy Training Center of Virginia
- Loudoun Association for Retarded Citizens

We agreed with Ms. Ruppmann's assessment and felt strongly that the due process decision under appeal in Loudoun County was Montgomery County's only motive to push for an injunction against us. During a press interview, Ms. Ruppmann said, "It should make no difference whatsoever to Montgomery County Schools in accepting Mark, but it means a lot to Loudoun County. Educators from Illinois have testified that Mark was successful in their inclusion program before the Hartmanns moved to Virginia. If Mark is successful in an inclusion program in Montgomery County, it blows Loudoun's case against the Hartmanns."

Mr. Bartlett, Jr. conveyed that Ms. Ruppmann's accusations were malarkey. While he rested his position solely on the legal issue of residency, however, it was obvious that other parents/children moving into Montgomery County had _not_ received this kind of treatment from Mr. Bartlett, Jr!

Another Day in Court

On February 16, 1995, we appeared in the Twenty-Seventh Judicial Circuit Court before Judge Ray W. Grubbs. Ms. Kimberly S. Ritchie, attorney at law, represented the Montgomery County School Board; Mr. Gerard Rugel represented us. Judge Grubbs held this hearing to decide whether he should grant a preliminary injunction prohibiting Mark's enrollment in the public schools of Montgomery County. After approximately three hours of testimony and legal argument, the court adjourned. Judge Grubbs did not rule from the bench, but rather indicated that his decision would be forthcoming.

Taking us totally by surprise, LCPS's next legal volley came in the form of a summons served to Joseph in Ashburn, Virginia on March 2, 1995, ordering him to appear in court on March 27th. The summons charged us with unlawfully failing to "cause Mark Hartmann to attend school on or about the 22nd of December, 1994; the 3, 4, 5, 6, 9, 10, 11, 12, 13, 17, 18, 19, 20, 23, 25, 26, 27, 30, and 31st of January 1995; the 1, 2, 3, 6, 7, 8, 10, 13, 14, 16, 17, 21, 22, 23, 24, 27, and 28th of February 1995; and the 1st of March 1995." The summons concluded, "This is against the peace and dignity of the Commonwealth."

Clearly, Loudoun County was intent on pursuing us down every possible legal path—and this particular initiative bordered on the absurd! The vindictiveness of leveling truancy charges became even more obvious in the face of LCPS's policy on home schooling. There were a significant number of children home schooled in Loudoun County whose parents receive little or no official resistance to this method of education. While these children fail to attend public school without incident, we were being *sued* over the matter!

Ironically, the tide in Montgomery County began to turn that same day. On March 2, 1995, Judge Grubbs issued his ruling on the preliminary hearing case, *Hartmann v. Montgomery County Public Schools* (27th Cir. 1995). Despite having residential addresses two hundred and fifty miles apart, Mark and Roxana were recognized as residents of Montgomery County! Judge Grubbs wrote:

> At this preliminary stage, the Court finds from the evidence as viewed in light of the relevant statute that Mark and his mother meet the residency provisions as set forth therein.
>
> This finding brings into focus the distinction as between domicile and residence. The state is silent as to any reference to domicile. Very simply said, domicile and residence are not equal, legal concepts. Their meaning is not legally equivalent. One may have only one domicile, but one may have more than one residence. It is apparent from the record that Mark and his mother are domiciled in Loudoun County. They are, however, residents of Blacksburg, Montgomery County, as well as Loudoun County. Their motive in moving to Montgomery County, as openly disclosed, is immaterial in establishing residency.

Roxana could now enroll Mark in a full inclusion program at Kipps E.S.

as planned!

On March 6, 1995, LCPS attorney, Ms. Mehfoud, pointed out in a letter to Mr. Rugel that because Mark was now officially a resident of Montgomery County, our appeal of the due-process decision in Loudoun County, also dated March 6th, should be withdrawn. In her letter, Ms. Mehfoud ominously wrote, "Failure to dismiss the appeal at this point will result in a request for attorney's fees on behalf of Loudoun, due to the Hartmanns' pursuit of a frivolous case."

Mark began third grade on March 8th as a student at Kipps E.S. The *Roanoke Times* quoted Roxana as follows: "Mark went straight to his desk, just as if he had always been there. He is now in the hands of people who know what to do. It's such a relief. I've longed for this day for so long."

On March 9th, Mr. Rugel responded to Ms. Mehfoud demanding that LCPS remove their truancy charges against us since Mark was now considered a resident of Montgomery County. In the same letter, he also cited the legal precedent within the Fifth Circuit Court of Appeals in Lee v. Biloxi as justification for our continued administrative appeal of the due process decision, commenting that "my reliance on the case can hardly be categorized as frivolous." Loudoun eventually dropped the truancy charges.

MCPS's legal machinations against us cost Mark more than five weeks of school as he waited from January 27th until he reentered third grade on March 8th. We consider Mr. Bartlett, Jr. to have acted as an ally of LCPS and not in the best interests of the citizenry of Montgomery County. In our opinion, his actions were shameful and bordered on an abuse of power.

Violation of Civil Rights?

We were contacted by an attorney in Blacksburg who had previously counseled us on Mark's enrollment in Montgomery County Public Schools and initially worked with Mr. Rugel to address MCPS's charges. In a March 14th letter, this attorney proffered that we might have a federal cause of action against MCPS on the grounds that the school board singled Mark out for scrutiny as a special-education student, although no other special-education students were treated similarly—thus violating Mark's civil rights. The attorney offered to represent us in this matter and to pursue reparation through federal court as opposed to the state court system.

Carefully reading the letter, we asked only one question: *Is this in Mark's best interest?* It didn't take us long to decide: We opted *not* to pursue legal action against Montgomery County Public Schools in a federal suit. After all, Mark was now in school at Kipps Elementary—happy—and supervised by caring and experienced professionals who knew how best to include him with his peers.

CHAPTER 15

ADMINISTRATIVE APPEAL PROCESS
Early 1995

During the first two months of 1995, in addition to representing us in court in Montgomery County, Mr. Rugel focused on reviewing the transcripts from the due-process hearing and deciding the best legal strategy for our administrative appeal.

On March 6th, in filing the administrative appeal of Ms. McBride's decision, Mr. Rugel wrote a fifteen-page brief on Mark's behalf that outlined our legal position. The following arguments are quoted from Mr. Rugel's brief:

A. A finding that Mark Hartmann did not benefit from his present placement does not require the hearing officer to also find that he <u>cannot</u> benefit from such a placement in the future.

The strong preference of the IDEA for placement in the regular classroom is rendered meaningless if a school system is permitted to place a student in a self-contained classroom as a result of its own failures.

B. The hearing officer failed to give due weight to Mark's success in the regular classroom during first grade.

C. Mark's failures to make academic progress resulted from a failure of implementation rather than the inappropriateness of his placement.

While a cursory review of the evidence might suggest that the school system provided Mark with sufficient supplementary aids and services, a more in-depth review demonstrates otherwise. Lacking an inclusion coordinator, Mark's teachers and his aide at Ashburn E.S. were left in the dark with respect to Mark's educational needs.

D. The decision to remove Mark from the regular education classroom after nine months was clearly premature.

This "rush to judgment" can be more easily understood if one considers the undue influence of Mr. Neil Winters, director of pupil services. Mr. Winters unequivocally opposed Mark's placement in the regular classroom. He was clearly in a position of power as evidenced by his unilateral decision to remove Ms. Meagan Kelly from involvement in Mark's program. Also, the IEP team wrote a new IEP on March 18th making no commitment to Mark's placement past May 31st, an action consistent with Mr. Winters' opposition to Mark's placement and contrary to administrative practice in Virginia. Regulations governing the development of IEPs call for the development of <u>annual goals and objectives</u>. If the team truly felt that Mark's placement was appropriate, they would have developed goals to be reviewed after one year, not two and one half months.

E. The hearing officer incorrectly found that Mark does not initiate social interactions and does not model his classmates.

To rebut this finding we have submitted a tape made by the school system that unambiguously shows Mark happily interacting in a playful manner with his classmates at Ashburn E.S. They are shown to respond in kind. In fact, as with many second graders, we observe the teacher asking Mark and his classmates to curb their playful activity.

F. The conclusion that Mark requires 1:1 to make academic gain does not require that he be placed in a self-contained program.

If Mark cannot derive academic benefit from the regular classroom, then Mark's IEP should be reconfigured to balance the amount of time that Mark can receive 1:1 attention for academics with a reasonable amount of time in the regular classroom for his social needs. This could be as simple as splitting his time 50% in 1:1 and 50% in the regular classroom at his neighborhood school.

G. Mark's presence in the classroom will not negatively impact his classroom.

What must be underscored is that the resolution of any behavioral problems lies in the appropriate adaptation of the curriculum coupled with a rational approach to behavior management. At best, the school system's approach to manage Mark's challenging behaviors was unthinking, haphazard and antiquated.

H. The proposed self-contained classroom does not provide for sufficient interaction with non-disabled peers.

We felt that these points appropriately summarized our position and called attention to some of the misguided conclusions made during the initial hearing. Thus, the administrative appeal was officially filed.

IEP – Kipps Elementary School

Meanwhile, during the IEP meeting on March 9, 1995, at Kipps Elementary School, Mr. Van Dyke, the principal, told Roxana that the focus of that IEP was to determine goals for both third and fourth grades for Mark. As such, Mr. Van Dyke commented that MCPS had begun interviewing prospective teaching assistants for Mark for fourth grade, and that he would ensure that they hired only the best candidates. He explained that during third grade, two teaching assistants would work with Mark, one in the morning and the other in the afternoon. Another child would share the teaching assistants with Mark. Indicating that this arrangement was very effective in the inclusion program, Mr. Van Dyke assured Roxana that both assistants would be fully trained and prepared to work with Mark. He said that Ms. Colley had a training program planned for newly hired teaching assistants and that she would coordinate closely with Roxana to arrange times for them to get to know Mark.

Mr. Van Dyke also planned for Ms. Colley to begin peer training as quickly as possible and welcomed Roxana to participate in the classroom discussions. Thus, it appeared that Kipps E.S. was on top of its responsibilities, showing refreshing energy in its attempts to transition Mark as smoothly as possible. For the first time since returning to Virginia, we felt at home. We never looked back!

Legal Opposition from LCPS

In her March 29th brief on behalf of LCPS and in opposition to our appeal, Ms. Mehfoud reiterated the school board's legal position. The program at Leesburg Elementary School, Mehfoud wrote, was the most beneficial for Mark plus it offered significant opportunities for mainstreaming with non-handicapped children. She contended that five days of testimony during the due-process hearing and the statements given under oath by twenty witnesses proved that LCPS's decision to change Mark's placement was a correct one. The following arguments are quoted from Ms. Mehfoud's brief:

> A. Inclusion in all regular classes is inappropriate for Mark Hartmann.
> B. Mark cannot learn only in a large class with distractions.
> C. The Loudoun staff was enthusiastic about inclusion and tried to make it succeed.

D. Mark requires placement in the autism program at Leesburg E.S.
E. Recent legal authorities support the hearing officer's decision.

Additionally, in her brief, Ms. Mehfoud contended that Mark was no longer entitled to a free and appropriate public education in Loudoun County because he was no longer a resident of that county. She presented arguments on the following legal points:

A. The IDEA requires that a student reside in the education authority's jurisdiction before any obligation to educate arises.
B. Virginia state law also requires residency before there is an obligation to educate.

Ms. Mehfoud's arguments contended that LCPS had gone above and beyond in its attempts to make full inclusion work for Mark. According to LCPS, Mark "received virtually no educational benefit in the included setting." His full-time presence in the classroom demanded a "disproportionate amount of the planning and classroom time of the regular teacher."

Concerning the administrative appeal, Ms. Mehfoud argued that the witnesses who testified at the due-process hearing were to be considered credible, while testimony taken from witnesses who had responded in writing and at our request did not carry sufficient weight to warrant consideration. Furthermore, Ms. Mehfoud argued that our appeal offered no new law or favorable arguments: "Their brief simply rehashes the arguments they presented unsuccessfully at the local due process hearing. These arguments did not prevail then and must not prevail on appeal...."

Then, Ms. Mehfoud turned to Mark's behaviors observed at Ashburn E.S., which, she asserted, "prohibited his complete inclusion in a regular classroom setting. These behaviors included continual vocalization, especially whining, screeching and crying when unhappy or frustrated, hitting, pinching, kicking, biting, sucking the leg of a chair, rolling on the floor, and removing his shoes and clothing. Mark is a big, strong child who cannot be easily restrained when he engages in injurious behaviors. He learns best when he is in a one-on-one situation and is hampered if there are any distractions. Mark exhibited no interest in his peers."

Ms. Mehfoud insisted that the faculty and staff at Ashburn E.S. had "worked intensively to make the inclusion successful for Mark." According to Ms. Mehfoud, "eight individuals within the school division and a number of consultants from outside the school division were involved in Mark's education."

Ms. Mehfoud felt that although we had asked for an inclusion facilitator, "it was established at the local hearing that there is no recognized educational position anywhere in Virginia known as an inclusion facilitator."

Finally, she concluded that since Mark was legally considered a resident of Montgomery County, the appeal should automatically be rendered null and void.

Our Response to LCPS

On April 4, 1995, Mr. Rugel responded to LCPS's brief opposing our appeal with a "reply brief on behalf of Mark Hartmann." The following excerpts capture the thrust of Mr. Rugel's arguments:

> The state reviewing officer is free to make a different conclusion of fact based on all the evidence, both testimonial and documentary. The court should consider two additional pieces of evidence. One was a videotape of Mark that showed his ability to interact with other children in a meaningful way. The other was the IEP developed by Montgomery County Public Schools for Mark that included, as in Loudoun County, a full-time aide. MCPS' IEP provided seven specific methods of accommodation to allow Mark to participate meaningfully in a regular classroom setting, however, as well as five annual goals and thirty-one short-term objectives. Unlike the educational program at Ashburn E.S., Mark would spend ninety-eight per cent of his time in a third-grade classroom with non-disabled peers.
>
> MCPS had also enlisted the aid of Ms. Kenna Colley who was an inclusion specialist within the MCPS system. Ms. Colley's testimony at the due-process hearing may not have carried the weight it should have because she was not working with Mark at that time. Now that she is working with Mark in Montgomery County, and participated in the development of Mark's current IEP, Ms. Colley's testimony should carry significantly more weight.
>
> The appeal was not moot because Mark was attending Montgomery County Public Schools. Mark still had a residence in Ashburn and if the Hartmanns decided to return Mark to the Loudoun County Public Schools, the same difficulties would be repeated. Under law, this possibility of repetition enabled our appeal to remain a viable legal action.

Results ... Administrative Review

May 1995 was anything but a time of reaffirmation and renewal. Mr. Alexander Simon, the hearing officer appointed to conduct the administrative appeal of the due process hearing, issued an eight-page decision on May 15, 1995.

Mr. Simon wrote, "After making an independent review of the record, I reach the same decision as that of the hearing officer in all respects, except that Loudoun County is directed to amend the May 31, 1994 IEP to provide Mark with adaptive physical education instruction in the regular physical education class at Leesburg Elementary School. I specifically approve the findings of fact and the legal analysis of the decision of the hearing officer."

In sum, Mr. Simon upheld Ms. McBride's due-process decision, and so, our administrative appeal of the due process proceedings came to a close. Mr. Simon's decision exhausted the remedies available to us through the Virginia public school system.

CHAPTER 16

THE LEGAL APPEAL PROCESS
1995

Weeks after Mr. Simon's decision, we called Mr. Rugel, conveying that Mark had finished out third grade at Kipps E.S. on a positive note. His IEP was set for the fall. We spoke nothing but praise for Ms. Kenna Colley, MCPS's inclusion specialist, and Mr. Ray Van Dyke, the principal of Kipps E.S. These two professionals had been the driving force behind a very positive and welcoming experience as Mark finished out the last weeks of third grade. Mark responded in kind, appearing comfortable and happy in his new school. Already, many of Mark's unwanted behaviors had diminished considerably, now that he was receiving structure, consistency, commitment to best practices, and understanding.

Given Mark's renewed success in an inclusion program and the exhaustion of state-level legal options, we decided to take our legal fight with Loudoun County Public Schools to the federal level.

By July 1st, we had met with Mr. Rugel to strategize the next step in our legal defense against LCPS. We decided to put the legal struggle on hold for a while to allow Mark time, during the fall, to adjust to his fourth grade placement at Kipps E.S. Hoping that Mark would experience success in that inclusive setting, we told Mr. Rugel that he should plan to file an appeal in the Federal District Court in Alexandria, shortly before the one-year deadline for filing an appeal expired, essentially before December 14, 1995. We were both confident that, by then, additional evidence from Mark's positive experience at Kipps E.S. in Blacksburg would be persuasive in federal court.

Growing Support

Shortly after making that decision, the Department for the Rights of Virginians with Disabilities (DRVD) informed Mr. Rugel that it had decided to support us with a stipend for legal representation if we decided to appeal our case to the federal level. When told of DRVD's decision, we were ecstatic and relieved that we were going to receive some help in the fight for Mark's education! The tide had begun to turn.

Later that summer, Mr. Rugel also received an offer of support from The Association of Severe Handicaps (TASH). Mr. Frank Laski, counsel to TASH who argued the OBERTI case in federal court, had contacted Mr. Rugel to offer legal assistance and educational expertise, if needed. We appreciated Mr. Laski's interest in our legal case and accepted his offer to provide an educational expert to testify in federal court on Mark's behalf.

By August 1995, Kipps E.S. had begun training Mark's new teacher's assistants for fourth grade, Ms. Diane Milburn and Mr. Greg Paynter. Both assistants held degrees in education and were aspiring primary school teachers. Roxana returned to Blacksburg to meet with the new assistants and introduce them to Mark. They planned out four or five half-days that Mark would come to school to work with them. A wonderfully relaxing time, Roxana enjoyed talking with Ms. Milburn and Mr. Paynter about Mark and his foibles. The teacher's assistants quickly became comfortable with Mark and learned to anticipate his reactions to the unexpected. Within weeks, Roxana judged that both had truly bonded with Mark.

Mark's fourth grade teacher, Ms. Beverly Strager, was also a consummate professional. She worked tirelessly in concert with Ms. Colley to implement fourth grade curriculum adaptations appropriate for Mark. Ironically, Ms. Strager found that some of those adaptations were also applicable to at least three other children who were having difficulty grasping the concepts being taught in her class.

While initially apprehensive about having Mark in her classroom, Ms. Strager learned that Mark was an affectionate boy who needed structure and consistency in his school day to learn best. Mark also required periodic movement breaks to decrease his anxiety level. This was easily accomplished by providing Mark ten minutes or so, each morning and afternoon, to go outside to swing by himself. The adaptations and accommodations developed by Ms. Colley for Ms. Strager's use in the classroom significantly helped Mark accomplish his IEP goals.

A New Challenge for Roxana

A mammogram in January 1995 showed that Roxana had fibrous tumors developing in her breasts. Follow-up sonograms confirmed several non-cancerous, fibrous tumors in each breast, but indicated nothing more serious. Deciding to have the tumors removed anyway, Roxana's outpatient surgery was scheduled for Friday, October 6, 1995. Laura and Joseph drove to Blacksburg on October 5th to be with Roxana and to care for her over the weekend.

Immediately following surgery, the surgeon asked to speak with Joseph. While he told Joseph that Roxana was in the recovery room doing well, the look on his face was worrisome. The surgeon then said that he had found a large, cancerous tumor in Roxana's right breast.

As the surgeon diagrammed the tumor's precise placement, Joseph's mind raced: *How had this tumor been missed, despite several mammograms and the ultrasound completed just prior to surgery?* The surgeon explained that the tissue density of the fibrous tumors was nearly identical to that of the cancerous tumor. So, in amidst the six non-cancerous fibroids, no one expected that he would find one cancerous tumor, 15 centimeters long. Joseph returned to the waiting room to tell Laura the news. They hugged and cried together, with thoughts focused on Roxana and her prognosis.

The laboratory results indicated that Roxana had two different types of cancer: the malignant tumor (infiltrating ductile carcinoma) in her right breast, and "non invasive intra-ductile carcinoma in situ" cells throughout her left breast. After consulting with the oncologist, we decided to have both breasts removed. The oncologist recommended a modified radical mastectomy on the right breast to remove the breast and lymph nodes, and a simple mastectomy on the left breast. These procedures were performed successfully on October 13, 1995.

On October 27th, we learned that five of the fifteen lymph nodes taken during the mastectomy contained cancer cells. This meant that the cancer had already spread beyond the lymph nodes into Roxana's body. Roxana's diagnosis was "stage 3 breast cancer." This was sobering and frightful—the oncologist gave Roxana a forty percent chance of living five years, even after treatment!

After receiving the laboratory results, the oncologist chartered a course of treatment that would include eight months of chemotherapy and seven weeks of radiation. Roxana decided to stay in Blacksburg for her treatments. Joseph took a temporary leave of absence from work and moved to Blacksburg to care for Roxana and manage Mark's school activities. Laura would spend the remainder of her sixth grade school year living with Joseph's older brother and sister-in-law in Green Bay, Wisconsin. Despite the gravity of Roxana's medical condition, our family once again pulled together to face the challenges ahead.

Federal Court Appeal

On December 6, 1995, Mr. Rugel filed our complaint against LCPS in the United States District Court in Alexandria, Virginia. Fundamentally, the suit was an appeal of the due process decision handed down in December 1994 by Ms. McBride in favor of LCPS. In the complaint, Mr. Rugel asserted that: LCPS refused to provide Mark with a free appropriate public education (FAPE) in the regular classroom; that LCPS had the duty to assure that children with disabilities and their parents are guaranteed procedural safeguards with respect to the provisions of a FAPE; and that LCPS deprived the IEP team of the ability to act independently, which violated those safeguards. Furthermore, Mr. Rugel charged that the State Review Officer's determination violated Mark's right to receive a free appropriate education as required by the IDEA and Section 504; and that, pursuant to those laws, LCPS must provide the plaintiff with a free appropriate public education in the regular education classroom.

In requesting relief, Mr. Rugel asked the Court to:

- Receive and review the administrative record and take additional evidence.
- Declare the right of the plaintiff (Mark Hartmann) to be provided with a FAPE in the regular education classroom by LCPS.
- Enjoin the defendants (LCPS) to develop and provide Mark Hartmann with a FAPE in the regular education classroom.
- Award the plaintiff reasonable attorneys' fees and costs pursuant to 20 U.S.C. #1415(4)B, for both this matter and the administrative proceedings from which this case is derived.

Within days of receiving the complaint, Ms. Mehfoud called Mr. Rugel to propose an out-of-court settlement. During the conversation, Ms. Mehfoud asked Mr. Rugel to send her a breakdown of the costs we had incurred to date relating to LCPS's due process procedure.

On December 11th, Mr. Rugel responded with a letter detailing $42,628 in costs, including $39,108 in attorney fees and other witness expenses/travel costs. In the letter, Mr. Rugel informed Ms. Mehfoud that his fees were now being paid by DRVD and, therefore, that the Hartmanns would not be personally burdened by increased legal expenses if the case was not settled. Finally, Mr. Rugel indicated that his fee would be substantially higher if we won the appeal and were awarded attorney's fees. He urged Ms. Mehfoud to encourage LCPS to settle the case, including full reimbursement of our expenses.

In response, Ms. Mehfoud made the following settlement offer in a letter to Mr. Rugel dated January 4, 1996. She wrote, "Please understand that the offer reflects a nuisance value for the suit, as I believe it is unlikely that the Court would overturn two adverse administrative decisions."

The offer was detailed as follows:

1. Payment of $10,000 in full settlement of the case.
2. Execution of a general release by the Hartmanns in favor of the School Board, its officers, agents, and employees releasing all matters accruing up to the date of the release.
3. Dismissal with prejudice of the case pending in federal court and withdrawal of any administrative complaints pending with federal, state or local authorities.
4. The Hartmanns also must agree that they will not file complaints in the future over any matters arising prior to the execution of the release.
5. Agreement by the Hartmanns that, if Mark is ever re-enrolled in the Loudoun County Public Schools, his current educational placement will be in a program similar to the one approved by the state review officer.
6. Confidentiality over the terms of the settlement.

While LCPS's offer of settlement was not unusual, the conditions attached to the settlement were especially damaging in this type of case. Notwithstanding, after a thorough collaborative review of our legal position, our equities in the case, and our circumstances in Blacksburg, Mr. Rugel responded in a letter dated January 10th that we would accept all of the terms except the offer of $10,000 payment, well below an acceptable amount. This was a difficult decision to make. At this juncture, we were satisfied that Mark was receiving an appropriate education in an inclusive setting–the least restricted environment–which was being implemented by a truly capable team of educators in Blacksburg. Additionally, DRVD had committed itself to shoulder the majority of our legal expenses to appeal the due process decision. Nonetheless, Roxana's fragile medical condition and prognosis were foremost in our minds. We wanted to put this distasteful legal experience behind us, if at all possible, and as quickly as it could be done, only if we could be restored financially. It was all about the *Hartmann family* returning to normal. We had exhausted our energies/resources at this point and were spent emotionally over what LCPS had done to us. On the positive side of the ledger, our fight for Mark's inclusion had risen to national prominence. We had made the most of media opportunities (television, newspapers, radio) to contrast the best practices in education with the failed special education programs of the 1970s, as forced upon us by LCPS. If we could, this was the moment to bow out of the fight.

Mr. Rugel wrote, "As you know, DRVD is funding this litigation and the Hartmanns have no additional financial liability. With no further economic risk, they are only willing to accept a settlement of $35,000 which will restore them financially."

To close, Mr. Rugel added, "I hope your client is fully aware that, aside from the real chance of losing this case, they will probably expend $35,000 in attorney fees and associated costs. We believe that those funds would be more appropriately paid to the Hartmanns, who after all are residents and taxpayers of Loudoun County forced to respond to the school system's request for due process."

LCPS responded by filing a motion to dismiss with the Federal District Court in Alexandria on February 2, 1996. In its motion, LCPS basically stated that Mark was no longer a resident of Loudoun County and, therefore, LCPS had no obligation to educate him. The school system reasoned that the complaint against LCPS was moot, since Mark's residency in Montgomery County implied the intention to stay there indefinitely. Thus, LCPS moved that our appeal should be dismissed.

A motion to dismiss is the type of legal action that a party makes prior to a trial date, essentially requesting that the court throw the case out without further deliberation because of an overwhelming fact or decisive principle of law. According to LCPS, the overwhelming fact in this case was that Mark no longer lived within that school system's jurisdiction.

In our brief response to LCPS's motion to dismiss, Mr. Rugel stated flatly, "Equity requires that the appeal in his case be heard." Among other arguments, he wrote:

> The Hartmanns, and similarly situated parents such as those in "Daniel R.R." and "Lee," are faced with agonizing decisions about the educational needs of their children. Here the Hartmanns assert that 1) the appropriate education for Mark requires that he be educated in a regular education classroom and 2) that LCPS has failed to provide the appropriate aids and supplementary services which would allow Mark to benefit from such a placement.
>
> The belief of Mr. and Mrs. Hartmann that their son can be educated in the regular classroom in a public school can only be demonstrated in a similar setting. In order to demonstrate that a well-designed program in the regular public school classroom can work for Mark, the Hartmanns, by necessity, have had to enroll their son in a public school outside of Loudoun County. It would be inequitable to dismiss this appeal as a result of the actions of LCPS, which have caused the Hartmanns to go outside of Loudoun County in order to provide an appropriate education for their son.

For the reasons stated above…, the instant case presents a live controversy and is not moot. The defendant's Motion to Dismiss should be denied.

On February 14, 1996, Loudoun County Public Schools and Ms. Mehfoud suffered their first defeat in the legal battle against us: LCPS's motion to dismiss was denied. With this, and our attempt to settle out of court stalled, our appeal would proceed to the federal level, as planned.

At Home In Blacksburg

Meanwhile, we adopted a routine centered on Mark's daily schooling and Roxana's chemotherapy treatments, which occurred every three weeks. Mark was doing well in school. His teacher's assistants felt comfortable with Mark and gradually began to fade away the level of support they provided him. Soon, before school started each day, Mark was independently taking down the chairs in the classroom and placing them squarely behind their respective desks. He was also in charge of the class calendar and, notably, never made a mistake.

Academically, Mark was scoring high on reading comprehension tests as well as in arithmetic. His favorite classes were social studies and library. In social studies, Mark frequently participated in a small work group that would present their work to the class. He especially enjoyed doing his part during those presentations.

In addition to swinging outside for movement breaks, Roxana suggested that Mark could also ride his bicycle, complete with training wheels, around the playground. Ms. Colley agreed, and soon Mark had his bicycle at school.

Roxana was concerned that, unless taught, Mark would never learn how to ride a bicycle without training wheels. After discussing the issue with Ms. Colley and Mr. Paynter, plans were made for Joseph to come to school each day to help Mark learn to ride his bike. At first, Mark resisted even getting on the bicycle because it no longer had training wheels. A kitchen timer was set for two minutes, and with Joseph on one side and Mr. Paynter providing reassurance from the other, we encouraged Mark to peddle his bicycle around the playground. After a week, Mark became accustomed to the routine, but it was slow going.

The bicycle-training time was stretched to five minutes, then to eight minutes and, finally, fifteen minutes. Gradually, Mr. Paynter and Joseph began fading away their support. Eventually, only one of them needed to run alongside Mark on his bike. He learned how to balance himself and, in the end, to ride—totally independently. In fact, this ultimately became one of Mark's favorite outdoor activities. We chuckle when we tell acquaintances that Mark is one of the few children in the world who learned how to ride a two-wheeled bicycle *without ever falling!*

CHAPTER 17

EXPERT WITNESSES
1995 - 1996

During April 1995, in preparation for the federal appeal, Mr. Frank Laski of TASH notified Roxana that Dr. Patrick Anthony Schwarz from Oak Park, Illinois was willing to work as an expert on Mark's behalf. He described Dr. Schwarz as a young, dedicated educator with a solid background. Dr. Schwarz earned his doctoral degree in special education/ educational administration at the University of Wisconsin in 1991.

According to Mr. Laski, Dr. Schwarz had been an expert witness in special education cases at least four times and knew the legal ropes well. Finally, Mr. Laski said that Dr. Schwarz had been a student under Dr. Lou Brown at the University of Wisconsin. We were delighted, as Dr. Brown was one of Roxana's favorites among educators advocating for the inclusion of children with disabilities.

As our expert witness, all agreed that Dr. Schwarz would need to spend time with Mark at school, at home, and in the community, so that he would have firsthand knowledge of Mark when giving testimony in court. Early May 1995 was targeted as the best time for Dr. Schwarz to come to Virginia to make his personal observations. Ideally, we would have had Dr. Schwarz spend time at Kipps E.S. in Blacksburg where Mark was currently enrolled, as well as time at Leesburg E.S. observing the autism program wherein LCPS proposed he attend. To our dismay, however, MCPS would not allow Dr. Schwarz to observe Mark in the actual classroom, nor interview Kipps E.S. staff on school grounds. Similarly for LCPS, MCPS would not allow LCPS representatives to observe Mark in class nor interview Kipps E.S. staff on school grounds in preparation for the anticipated court battle, either. Clearly, MCPS did not want to become involved in any way with the legal battle that was about to ensue.

Seeking an alternative to direct classroom observation, we asked a neighborhood friend to videotape Mark at school, in preparation for

Dr. Schwarz's visit. Permitted two filming days, we decided to have Mark videotaped from the time he got off the bus until lunch, on the first day—and from lunch through the end of the school day, on the second day.

We instructed our neighbor that the video had to be non-stop, for the entire three-plus hours. While physically draining to hold the camera that long each day, this resulted in an excellent, representative sample of Mark's day at school, including his fourth-grade activities, classroom work, and peer interaction.

Joseph met Dr. Schwarz upon his arrival to the Roanoke Airport on May 1st. He was enthusiastic about working with us and wanted to see all six hours of videotape, the very night he arrived. Dr. Schwarz deemed this significant preparation for his discussions with Ms. Colley, Roxana and Joseph, and for his first meeting with Mark, the next day.

During three days of consultation (one day in Blacksburg and two days in Leesburg and Herndon), Dr. Schwarz observed Mark in various settings outside of school, talked extensively with us, interviewed Ms. Colley, and met with Ms. Ruppmann and Mr. Rugel. Additionally, he reviewed select documents from the due process hearing, analyzed Mark's current IEP, and spent four hours observing the autism program at Leesburg E.S. (along with Mr. Jernigan who was serving as a witness for LCPS).

Subsequently, Dr. Schwarz wrote an independent evaluation reporting on his observations, outlining the data collected, and providing his overall analysis and conclusions. In effect, the report would serve as a mnemonic for Dr. Schwarz during his testimony in the Federal District Court of Appeals in Alexandria. This report was also submitted to the court as an exhibit supporting our legal position.

The following excerpts are taken from Dr. Schwarz's report:

Current Educational Placement

Two representative half-day videotapes (one a.m. & one p.m.) were viewed in their entirety to partially evaluate Mark Hartmann's current educational placement. Mark receives support from a team of people primarily including one general education teacher, one special education teacher, two teacher assistants (one a.m. & one p.m.), a speech and language therapist and an occupational therapist. Mark also receives some individualized support in the areas of mathematics, speech, and occupational therapy. Some major areas of focus in Mark's education include:

Communication

A total communication approach is utilized. Mark is encouraged to communicate through a variety of methods: pointing to picture symbol board, vocalizations, using the Canon Communicator, computer keyboard, gestures and facial expressions. Mark keeps his picture symbol board with him at all times, so he always has the opportunity to communicate and make choices at any given time.

Reciprocal Interactions

Mark has close physical proximity to his chronological age peers the majority of his school day. When school activities call for peers to work with one another, Mark also works in a group. Mark was observed in a reading activity with a peer. She read a story and he followed along with his finger. Mark has reading skills and this type of activity was beneficial for both students. According to Ms. Colley, Mark is also increasing eye contact to his peers. When students get to choose partners for activities, it is typical that Mark has many children who want to be with him. Mark is also having significant reciprocal interactions with adult professionals.

Academic Skills

Mark has emerging language and literacy skills. He is vocalizing words periodically, such as "yes," "no," "snow," etc. When Mark is encouraged to vocalize words, he will do so with a familiar person. Mark has good basic mathematics skills and demonstrated competency in the areas of addition, geometry, money and time. Since Mark is in the general education classroom for the majority of his day, the general curriculum is always referenced, so Mark is always encouraged to gain skills in a systematic grade level fashion. Mark is attending to his tasks and responsibilities and following directions.

Choice

When Mark utilizes his current picture board, he is able to identify feelings and make choices. This is extremely important for an intelligent student with autism who is non-verbal. There were many opportunities during the course of Mark's school day for him to make choices.

Movement

Movement breaks are incorporated into Mark's school day. The theory of sensory integration indicates that movement opportunities for many students with autism may be beneficial in their learning. Movement breaks for Mark are implemented in a normalized manner. Mark has two breaks during which he goes to the playground to swing and ride a bicycle. Mark also has responsibilities during the school day, which give him additional movement opportunities. He has to take down all the chairs in the classroom at the beginning of the school day. He also has to pick up the mail for a staff member. These responsibilities assist Mark in developing a work ethic, which is critically important for all students, including children with disabilities.

Findings and Recommendations

1.   Mark is proceeding exceptionally well in his general education classroom and there is significant educational benefit. He is in proximity of, and reciprocally interacting with, other students and adults. Mark's academic skills are quite impressive for a student with autism. Mark is improving reading and spelling skills. Mark utilizes computer-based instruction in settings with his general education peers. He is answering questions utilizing the computer. Staff professionals working with Mark report gains across the board in all IEP areas. From my review of Mark's current IEP, he is not only meeting educational goals and objectives, but also exceeding them.

2.   Most interfering actions that have been listed on previous reports were not seen in the video representing a full school day. Ms. Colley has reported that Mark's interfering actions are fairly minor as compared to when he first came to the school and was upset. The staff has a back up plan for any interfering actions that may occur and have achieved success through this system. We cannot underestimate the positive influence of the inclusive model on Mark's behavior. He is in a situation where he is with the best of student models and does not have to compete with other students to "outdo" each other with interfering actions. Staff members always look at the communicative meaning for all of Mark's actions and that is one of the keys in successfully educating him.

3.   Mark's current special educator, Ms. Colley, is extremely versed in current methodology for inclusion. She understands how to collaboratively plan with her professional team to create curricular adaptations. She promotes multi-level instruction (teaching students at differing ability levels) in the general education classroom. She is always seeking out ways to showcase Mark's abilities and work. She assesses students using curricular, qualitative types of measures,

curricular-based assessment, MAPPING (Forest & Lusthaus, 1990), and videotaping, which is strongly recommended in the educational field for <u>all students</u>.

4.   It is my opinion that Mark has greater academic skills and potential than anyone has given him credit for having. Most standardized test measures rely on verbal responses, and since Mark's communication systems are currently being broadened, his skills are not being entirely represented, as is the case for many students with disabilities. As his team explores communication options, they will discover more academic skills. Obviously, Mark understands significant oral language. I observed him following many directions given by adults and students in general education settings and during individual sessions. Mark is learning many academic skills, acceptable behaviors and responsibility that will prepare him for the future real world in normalized settings.

Proposed Educational Placement

The self-contained classroom for students with autism was observed at Leesburg E.S. in Leesburg, Virginia for four hours. There were six children enrolled in the classroom, between kindergarten and fourth grade. Other environments that were different than the self-contained classroom were observed. All students were observed at a separate recess that was not on the general playground, but rather in the school courtyard, where perhaps the general kindergarten children have recess. One child was observed for a few minutes in a general kindergarten setting. Two children were observed during mainstreaming into a general education physical education class. Two other children were observed during mainstreaming into a general education music class.

Classroom Activities

Staff was making an effort to keep three of the six students occupied. The focus of the program was on one-on-one individualized instruction. There was one teacher, Ms. Emily LaCombe, and two teacher assistants present in the room for the majority of the time. At any given time in the classroom, three students received individualized instruction and the other three were allowed to take a break within the room. The break activities included the use of a net swing, movement around the room and sitting on a beanbag chair. Also, a speech and language clinician, Ms. Cristina Conroy-Winters, was present in the room for thirteen minutes.

There was a bulletin board in the classroom that read "Job Board," however, it was the schedule of activities based on the IEP for each student in the classroom. A typical schedule included most of the following activities:

Calendar	Spelling	Reading	
Recess	Math	All About Me	
Snack	Self Help	Coins	
Time	Physical	Bus	
Music	Education	Lunch	PlayDough

Students engaged in these activities while they were at tables or on the floor in the classroom.

Playground

Playground activities included running around the playground, playing on playground equipment for very young children and using hula-hoops. Each child engaged in a separate activity. None of the children played together. The students who were not engaged in self-stimulating behaviors such as flapping arms were with two different teacher's assistants and the teacher.

Speech and Language

Ms. Conroy-Winters came to the classroom to work with one student on a communication board. After thirteen minutes of focused work, she put away the student's communication system, and was not seen again for the rest of the afternoon.

Mainstreaming

Three mainstreaming environments were observed. The first environment was in a general kindergarten setting. The mainstreamed girl stayed in the class for approximately five minutes of a story time. When the teacher's assistant announced in a voice all students could hear, "she's messed her pants so she has to go back," the mainstreamed girl had to return to her self-contained classroom. The next environment was in a physical education class in which two male students were present with a teacher's assistant for part of the class. There was a substitute present and the students were working on personal exercises that were assigned by the instructor. There was also another boy with a disability who was present in the class, from a different self-contained classroom base. The students were asked to number off by the teacher so they could form groups. Since the three students with disabilities were all seated together, they all had different numbers. One teacher's assistant made an attempt to arrange the first boy in his assigned line with the students who were his non-disabled peers. When the other boys were called to be in their assigned lines, the second teacher's assistant thought it would be easier to create a separate special education line comprised with all students who had disabilities. As such, there was no attempt to integrate the students with autism together with their peers without disabilities. The third environment was in a music class, in which two other male students were present. Students in this class were being instructed to play simple chords and strum on the guitar. One boy walked around the room with his guitar. Another boy sat on the lap of the teacher's assistant in a rocking chair.

Findings and Recommendations

1. It was very difficult for me to ascertain the responsibilities of students and the schedule in the classroom. Students were engaged in any given activity from one to thirteen minutes. At least half of the class at any given time was engaged in down time. The "classes" that were truly activities did not reference a grade level general education schedule. Students worked on play dough at one table; on letters and numbers at another table; and on matching and sequencing on the floor.

2. Students were allowed to engage in running and self-stimulating behaviors within the self-contained classroom at great length. There was a boy and a girl who would run around the room flapping their arms and making noises. In my opinion, they were trying to outdo each other with unacceptable behaviors. There were no models of acceptable behavior in this classroom.

3. This program has failed miserably in addressing the most important need areas for students with autism: communication, reciprocal interactions, and choice making. Not one time during the entire afternoon did I see reciprocal interactions or choice making being taught, facilitated, or encouraged. Everything was set up so students would work in isolation of others, all the time, even on the playground. Not one student had a communication system that was with him/her at any time during the four hours I observed. The only time I saw a communication system utilized was when Ms. Conroy-Winters walked in with a system for a male student, worked with him for thirteen minutes, and put it away. This is equivalent to taking away a voice from a person who speaks and only giving them the opportunity to speak for thirteen minutes per

day. This particular student did not reciprocally speak words, so he was in desperate need of a communication system, as were all the other students in the room. There was one boy in the classroom that said some words sometimes, but he never answered questions or engaged in a conversation with anyone. He was in dire need of a communication system. Since autism, by current definition, is a communication and social disorder, I find the fact that this program did not even minimally address these areas, inexcusable.

4. I wanted to see if the students were capable of reciprocal interactions, so during recess I started to roll a hula-hoop near one of the older boys with autism. He watched me for a while, and then tried to do the same. He rolled it to me upon request. He also retrieved a hula-hoop at my request. Students were capable of having reciprocal interactions, but they were not arranged, taught or encouraged at any time.

5. During the time I observed students in the three mainstream environments, I never saw any student without a disability greet or talk to any of the students with autism. Adults did not facilitate communication, reciprocal interactions and choice making. The students with autism were barely seen as visitors, and certainly were not treated as members of the classes. It appeared that these opportunities do not happen often, or if they do, the staff people that were present in the mainstreaming settings were never trained or shown strategies to facilitate the students with autism to be contributing and participating members of the class. Since communication was not even addressed, the students with autism had no clue about their responsibilities and expectations in the class. The teacher's assistants that were present with the mainstreamed students created separate segregated subgroups for the students with autism. In the physical education class, the teacher's assistant did not support students with autism to be in their assigned line with the other students; rather, she created a separate special education line. In music class, the teacher's assistant allowed the boy to sit on her lap in a rocking chair, when the rest of the students were working on their guitars, seated on the floor. In the self-contained classroom before the music class, this same boy was on the floor and this demonstrated he was very capable of doing this. Normalization was never the focus. Students were not being prepared to function in the real world.

6. For any interfering action, teaching staff must ask the question, "What is the communication intent of the behavior?" rather than placing blame wholly on the student. It is my professional opinion

that the staff in the self-contained classroom viewed interfering behaviors as problems rather than communication. This was evident since there was not a single student who utilized a communication system that they kept with them throughout the time they were observed. Therefore, the students in this self-contained classroom will always be seen as separate and segregated since they have no voice with others.

7. There was no evidence of the curricular materials that teachers use for general education within the self-contained classroom. Instead, the materials were entirely separate from the general education curriculum and did not reference any grade level norm. There was a net swing in the middle of the classroom and a child's pool full of materials. The other classrooms for students without disabilities did not have these types of materials. There is a triple strike against the students with autism in this school ever getting into general education. First, grade level materials were not used. Second, normalization was not promoted. There were regular swings available on the general playground for vestibular sensory integration movement. Third, since students were not being taught to communicate and socialize, they will always be outside the norm in this school.

8. The last time that I viewed a program for students with autism that was similar to this program was in Madison, Wisconsin at the Metropolitan School District in 1981. I was a student teacher in a self-contained classroom for students with autism in an elementary school. There were major differences though. We facilitated choice making for students in Madison. All students had a communication system in Madison. Reciprocal interaction training was embedded in the program curriculum in Madison. This was considered an exemplary program at the time, and Dr. Anne Donnellan, who is considered a national expert in autism, supervised it. A lot has happened in the field of special education for students with autism since that time, and this program in Madison looked different even by 1983. The current program in Leesburg has not kept up with even minimal best practices for educating students with autism. I would estimate this program to look like typical programs for students with autism taking place in the late seventies, so it is almost twenty years behind the times in educational practices for students with autism.

Home and Community Functioning

Mark was observed during dinner time and evening time up until bedtime within his home setting. Mark was also observed eating and socializing in a restaurant with friends, shopping in a neighborhood grocery store, playing in a community park, riding in a car and proceeding on foot through an airport.

Mark has many responsibilities at home for setting the table, cleaning up and doing dishes. He earns money based on the number of dishes he washes. Mark also is quite independent with personal hygiene. These skills will serve him well as an adult.

Mark blended nicely into the community restaurant, the grocery store and the park. He had a grand time with his friends in the restaurant and was entirely comfortable. Mark enjoyed getting out and finding ways to occupy his time. Again, his family has given him many opportunities to be part of the community. The community skills he has learned have complemented nicely with his expectations and responsibilities within the school setting.

Summary

There are many examples of school districts across the country, which are educating students who have more severe autism than Mark has in general education classrooms. The two major classrooms that were evaluated for this report were dramatically different in their approach. Mark's present placement is addressing his educational, academic, behavioral and social needs splendidly and is preparing him and his peers for the future. He is making gains and surpassing objectives in all IEP areas. Our world does not contain one type of person, but rather there is great diversity in our communities. Our classrooms should reflect our neighborhoods and communities, and embrace diversity.

Mark has been educated within inclusive education environments his entire life. He has had successful programs in Lombard, Illinois and currently in Blacksburg, Virginia. There are some school districts in our country that have not given their teachers the knowledge, tools, training and philosophical base to educate students in a diverse, inclusive model. When this is the case in a school district, the student should not be blamed when there are difficulties that may be due to lack of staff training and experiences.

If Mark was taken from his inclusive fourth grade classroom in Blacksburg and placed in the self-contained classroom for students with autism in Leesburg, in my professional opinion he would lose the following:

• A normalized schedule where classes begin and end
• Age appropriate peer models

- A focus on total communication skills across all environments
- Opportunities to socialize - this is difficult to accomplish with six people who are non-verbal
- Reciprocal interactions with others
- Choice-making opportunities
- Learning lifelong skills in normalized environments
- Development of a work ethic - attending to task, following directions, increasing the amount of time on work, quality of work
- Age appropriate curricular activities and materials
- Routine models (e.g. Mark learned how to throw away his lunch bag by being with non-disabled peers at lunch)
- A promising future in a diverse, progressive community that values individual differences
- After all, **we all have individual differences and they should be valued and celebrated**.

After reading Dr. Schwarz's report, we knew that we had made the right decision in relying upon Mr. Laski and TASH to recommend an expert. We were literally breathless that someone else saw our educational concerns so clearly and, through his observations, could so effectively portray the differences in educational philosophy between LCPS and us. We were ecstatic about Dr. Schwarz's findings and with the clarity he brought to the legal arguments over Mark's education.

Preparing for Court – Again

By May 24, 1996, Mr. Rugel finished compiling an affidavit that addressed the fourteen interrogatories asked by LCPS in its preparation for court. Ms. Mehfoud had to respond to four interrogatories that we required for our preparation. In addition, Ms. Mehfoud asked to depose the witnesses from Kipps E.S. who had been working with Mark in fourth grade. The depositions were taken in Blacksburg, with Ms. Mehfoud extensively questioning each witness. We had to sit quietly during the depositions, while it appeared to us that Ms. Mehfoud's purpose was more to rattle the Kipps staff rather than to gain any insight into the truth of their testimony.

According to his strategic plan, Mr. Rugel would focus on testimony from four witnesses to present our federal case of appeal:

- Dr. Patrick Schwarz would testify to the observations and opinions set out in his expert witness report.
- Ms. Kenna Colley would testify to the professional observations and opinions set out in her summary report on the progress of Mark's inclusion program. The grounds for Ms. Colley's opinions were her personal observations of Mark, made in her capacity as inclusion specialist since first meeting Mark in June 1994.
- Ms. Beverly Strager, Mark's fourth grade regular education teacher, would testify to her work with Mark in the classroom. Ms. Strager would also address the curriculum modifications and adaptations used to involve Mark in planned classroom activities.
- Mr. Greg Paynter would testify to the current educational program for Mark at Kipps E.S. As teacher's assistant, Mr. Paynter had developed a productive working relationship with Mark and worked directly with him on academic areas such as science, social studies, reading, motor activities (bike riding), and communication (using augmentative communication devices).
- Joseph was asked to testify to the contentious and adversarial nature of our interactions with LCPS from the time that LCPS decided to take us to due process until Christmas vacation, 1994.

Following the filing of the proposed findings of fact and conclusions of law presented by both parties, the stage was set for the actual federal court trial. The court date was set for Monday, September 9, 1996.

CHAPTER 18

BRINKEMA'S DECISION
Late 1996

Alexandria, Virginia is the home of the United States District Court for the Eastern District of Virginia. Ironically, the judge appointed to hear our appeal, the Honorable Leonie M. Brinkema, is the parent of a child diagnosed with Down Syndrome. Unlike the vision that we held for Mark's education, Judge Brinkema had chosen a special education classroom for her own child's schooling. Before the proceedings began, Judge Brinkema felt compelled to make us aware of her own personal circumstances and then asked, in case of any conflict of interest, if we would want her to excuse herself from the proceedings. We responded that we did not.

As part of the procedural rule for an appeal of a lower court's decision, we were allowed to present evidence at the appeal that was not presented during the due-process hearing. Relevance was the only criteria for new evidence. In our case, because education is not a frozen moment in time, it was correctly argued that Mark's program at Kipps E.S. was relevant to deciding the merit of LCPS's proposed placement for Mark in the autism program at Leesburg E.S. Judge Brinkema ruled that the new evidence would be allowed. She watched and listened carefully to the videotaped segments of Mark at Kipps E.S. in Blacksburg, and listened carefully to testimony from both sides of the courtroom.

Mr. Rugel submitted the entire six hours of videotape showing Mark at Kipps Elementary School as evidence to support our legal argument. After nearly two full days of testimony, both sides rested. It was now up to Judge Brinkema to make her decision. We would not have long to wait.

Judge Brinkema's Decision

On November 27, 1996, Judge Brinkema issued her decision. It was the day before Thanksgiving. Here follows Judge Brinkema's decision in

Hartmann v. Loudoun County Board of Education, Civil Action 95-1686 A. (U.S. D.C. Va. 1996). (Author's note: Once again, the following text is not intended to be redundant for the reader, but rather is provided to illustrate the judge's reasoning behind her decision.)

To paraphrase an education commercial, "A mind is a terrible thing to waste." The challenge presented in this lawsuit ultimately focuses on just this concern. The issue is whether Mark Hartmann, an autistic eleven-year-old boy, should be educated in a regular education classroom which will expose him to a full range of academic subjects and allow him to interact with non-disabled children or be educated in a separate setting which will stress life skills over academic subjects and keep Mark with other disabled children for a significant portion of the day. This dispute pits Mark's parents, educators from Montgomery County, Virginia, and inclusion advocates against the Loudoun County Board of Education and some teachers who have worked with Mark.

Having carefully reviewed transcripts of the five-day due process hearing, the opinion of the Hearing Officer, the testimony presented before this Court in a two-day bench trial and the videotape showing two of Mark's school days in the Montgomery County, Virginia school system, the Court is convinced that Mark is able to receive significant educational benefits when included in a regular education setting as long as he has the help of a one-on-one aide and properly adapted curriculum. The Court also finds that when Mark is managed properly he is no more disruptive than his non-disabled classmates are. Lastly, the Court finds that the Hearing Officer failed to consider extensive evidence showing that Mark can learn when included in the regular setting. Therefore, the decision of the Hearing Officer is reversed and judgment is entered in favor of the plaintiffs.

I. Procedural Background

The parents of Mark Hartmann ("Mark") have brought this lawsuit...to ask the Court to reverse the findings of a due process Hearing Officer who concluded that the Loudoun County Board of Education ("the Board") had established that Mark could not be educated satisfactorily when he received all, or almost all, of his instruction in a regular education classroom, even with the use of supplementary aids and services. She also concluded that the Board's plan to place Mark in a self-contained autism class, located in a regular education school thereby providing opportunities for interaction with non-disabled peers, was appropriate and constituted the least restrictive educational environment for Mark.

At the outset, the Board opposed this lawsuit by arguing that it should be deemed moot because at the present time Mark is not being educated in Loudoun County. Rather than acquiescing to Loudoun County's decision, Mrs. Hartmann established residence in Montgomery County, Virginia, where Mark is presently enrolled in public school. Mr. Hartmann, however, continues to reside in Loudoun County; therefore, Mark remains eligible to attend school in Loudoun County. The parents have also stated they would re-enroll Mark if he were included in a regular classroom setting. Under these facts, the Court found that the core issues of this action are not moot because the problem is capable of repetition.

The Board also opposed the Court conducting a trial, arguing that the Court should base its decision solely on an evaluation of the adequacy of the due process hearing administrative record. However, the Court is required to make a "bounded, independent" decision in this case, "bounded by the administrative record and additional evidence, and independent by virtue of being based on a preponderance of the evidence before the court." The evidence presented during the two-day trial was extremely relevant to evaluating the adequacy of the Hearing Officer's decision, and has played a significant role in the Court's decision. Receipt of such evidence is appropriate under the IDEA, 20 U.S.C. - 1415(e)(2).

Lastly, the Board argues that the Hearing Officer's decision was fully supported by the record and should not be overturned. It is this issue, which will be addressed in detail in this opinion....

II. The Hearing Officer's Findings

In evaluating the educational program and placement proposed by the Board, the Hearing Officer considered two issues: 1) whether the proposal to remove Mark from the regular classroom violates the Board's obligation to educate him, to the maximum extent appropriate, with non-disabled children; and 2) whether the proposed placement in a self-contained class is appropriate for Mark....

The IDEA also contains a requirement that states establish "procedures to assure that, to the maximum extent appropriate, children with disabilities are educated with children who are not disabled, and that special classes, separate schooling, or other removal of children with disabilities from the regular education environment occurs only when the nature or severity of the disability is such that education in regular classes with the use of supplementary aids and services cannot be achieved satisfactorily." It is clear from the language of the statute that there is a strong presumption favoring the education of disabled children in the regular education environment, alongside children who are not disabled.

Within this statutory framework, the Hearing Officer found on the first issue that the Board had met its burden of establishing...that its proposal to remove Mark from the regular classroom did not violate its obligation to educate him...with non-disabled children....

The Hearing Officer found that Mark cannot be educated satisfactorily when he receives all, or almost all, of his instruction and related services in the regular classroom, even with the use of supplementary aids and services. The factors used to make this finding were: the steps that the school had taken to try to include Mark in a regular classroom, a comparison between the educational benefits of the segregated, special education classroom, and the effects of including Mark on the regular classroom environment.... Although the Board made reasonable efforts to accommodate Mark in the regular classroom, he received virtually no educational benefit in the included setting and that Mark's behaviors were disruptive and had a negative effect on the environment in the classroom.

The Hearing Officer also found that the Board's proposal for a self-contained program which allowed for mainstreaming in all non-academic activities gave Mark a significant opportunity to interact with non-disabled peers on a regular and daily basis, while offering him academic instruction and related services in a manner from which he would derive educational benefit.

III. Analysis

At the onset of this analysis, the Court must stress what this case is <u>not</u> about. Although seen by some as a battle between proponents of inclusion and separation, this case is solely about what is in the best interests of one disabled boy. The answer for Mark does not necessarily mean that the same answer would be appropriate for all other autistic children. The wisdom behind the IDEA is its unwavering focus on the individual disabled child and his or her unique challenges and needs. This Court has no doubt that specialized centers and separate self-contained classes may be the least restrictive educational environments for some children whereas inclusion may be the answer for others. Thus, this decision is in no way meant to reflect the Court's view of the adequacy of the self-contained autism class at Leesburg Elementary School or at any other school. The decision in this case is limited solely to what is most appropriate for Mark Hartmann.

A. Obligation to Educate with Non-disabled Children

Although the Court finds that the Hearing Officer used the proper analytical framework to evaluate the Board's placement decision, the evidence in the administrative record, augmented by the evidence presented at trial, supports a different conclusion. The Board's proposal to remove Mark from the regular classroom did violate its obligation to educate him, to the maximum extent appropriate, with non-disabled children because the greater weight of the evidence establishes that Mark can receive and has received educational benefits when included in a regular classroom with the use of supplementary aids and services.

1. Reasonable Efforts to Accommodate

Although the Board initially made efforts to accommodate Mark's placement in a regular education classroom, these efforts were not sufficient to discharge its obligation under the IDEA. In the spring of 1993, the Hartmanns notified the school system that they were considering moving to Loudoun County, Virginia. (Transcript, Oct. 27 at 276.).... The Hartmanns forwarded Mark's educational records at this time. In June of 1993, the principal of Ashburn Elementary School, Lynn Meadows, approached a second grade teacher, Debra Jarrett, and asked whether she would be interested in having Mark join her class. Jarrett indicated that she would be interested. (Tr. Aug. 15 at 106.) The record shows that there was some confusion during the summer months as to whether the Hartmanns would actually move into Loudoun County. (Tr. Sept. 26 at 194, 232.) Jarrett, a regular education teacher, was not notified until the end of August that Mark would indeed be included in her class. (Tr. Aug. 15 at 105.) Although Jarrett had almost no experience dealing with autistic children, she was not offered any substantial training in autism or in the inclusion process. (Tr. Aug. 15 at 107.) However, she was given help in accommodating Mark by having her class size reduced to a total of 21 students. Also, a full-time aide was hired to work with Mark. (Tr. Sept. 26 at 194-97.) The record does not reveal the aide's qualifications.

Meagan Kelly, the Loudoun County Director of Special Education, was appointed to head the inclusion efforts. (Tr. Oct 27 at 280-

83.) Kelly was chosen because of her experience with the Virginia Systems Change Project, a program in which she received training in inclusion. (Tr. Oct. 27 at 278.) She also had some experience in developing educational programs for students who had been diagnosed with autism. (Tr. Oct. 27 at 279.) Kelly was in charge of training the staff that would be working with Mark. This group became Mark's IEP team....

Initially, Mark's IEP team included his classroom teacher, Debra Jarrett; his teacher's aide; the school principal, Lynn Meadows; and a speech and language pathologist, Cristina Conroy. None of them had any extensive experience working with an included autistic student. Their training in inclusion was limited to a one-day conference given by the Virginia Council for Administrators of Special Education. This team was charged with the responsibility of coordinating and implementing Mark's placement. Although the Hearing Officer found this team adequate, the Court rejects that conclusion. Autism is far too complex a disability, and the inclusion of autistic children is too challenging a project, to leave to persons lacking adequate training and experience. Mark's failure to function well at Ashburn is strong proof of the inadequacy of the training and experience of Mark's IEP team.

During the fall, Kelly arranged for the IEP team to receive outside consultations from educational consultants Jamie Ruppmann and Gail Mayfield. Both of these consultants had experience in the areas of autism and inclusion. According to Ruppmann's testimony, Kelly was concerned that the individuals on Mark's IEP team did not have sufficient experience with the challenge of including a disabled student such as Mark. Kelly asked Ruppmann to observe Mark in the regular education classroom, participate in the IEP meetings and offer suggestions to the IEP team. Ruppmann worked with the IEP team from November 2 to December 8, 1993. Mayfield visited Ashburn Elementary in November of 1993. Apparently, she gave advice regarding Mark's inclusion program, but she did not make an official report. Because Mayfield did not testify at the due process hearing and neither side offered any evidence from her, the value of her insights is not available. Only Ruppmann's testimony is in the record.

Kelly also involved Fred Jernigan, Loudoun County's Supervisor of Special Education. Although Jernigan had some experience working with autistic children in the 1970s, he had no experience working with an autistic child in a regular classroom setting. Jernigan became informally involved with Mark's placement during the first half of the year. Although Jernigan did not attend meetings with the IEP team or observe Mark during this time, he did make himself available by phone to offer advice on how to develop strategies for dealing with Mark's behavior.

The record before the Hearing Officer shows that Kelly was concerned about the lack of experience of Mark's IEP team and tried to provide supplementary aids and services. Her efforts ceased, however, when she was removed from her supervisory role on Mark's IEP team in early December of 1993. The decision was announced at the December 8, 1993 IEP meeting. This meeting is a critical event in this case. There is some secrecy surrounding exactly what happened during the meeting. It is clear, however, that NeilWinters, Director of Pupil Services, attended the meeting and that after this meeting Meagan Kelly was no longer in a supervisory role on the IEP team and Jamie Ruppmann was no longer called in by the Board to participate in the IEP meetings.

Changes to the IEP team continued in 1994. Fred Jernigan took on a more official role in January. He started to attend the weekly meetings and developed a behavior modification plan for Mark. Valerie Mason, a special education teacher, was added to the team late in February, with little more than three months remaining in the school year. Mason had experience in implementing inclusion placements for preschool programs and providing one-on-one special education services in the regular classroom. Apparently she did not have experience with including children of Mark's age group. Mason testified that when she began working with Mark, she was also training the classroom teacher and the aide in methods of working with him. With just three months left in the school year, it was apparent that the individuals working with Mark still did not have sufficient training to give his placement a fair chance.

The Hartmanns point to the changes made to the IEP team as clear evidence that the Board was not strongly committed to inclusion. The Board counters that argument by pointing to, among other evidence, Jernigan's testimony that at the time he was added to the IEP team, "staff from all over the county (was) involved in working with Mark to the point where the teachers felt like they were overloaded." Although the Court finds these efforts laudable, they were insufficient.

The Court finds that the changes to the make-up of Mark's IEP team are evidence of the inadequacy of the Board's efforts to accommodate Mark in an inclusive setting. Meagan Kelly has testified that before and after the December IEP meeting she was committed to inclusion for Mark. She made efforts to provide adequate services to make Mark's placement a success. Jamie Ruppmann testified that Mark's needs are best met in an inclusive setting because, among other considerations, he would benefit from being around normal verbal children. Ruppmann was in favor of inclusion for Mark. She worked closely with the IEP team during the first half of the school year and continued to provide support afterwards when the Hartmanns hired her as their educational advocate. Moreover, Jernigan appears to the Court to be a philosophical opponent of inclusion. He testified in regards to Mark's academic progress, "I think there has been no progress academically in the inclusive settings. I see no evidence in the record that there's any progress whatsoever."

It is obvious that by the middle of the school year, the Board had decreased its efforts to make Mark's inclusion program successful. The record before the Hearing Officer demonstrates how Mark's behavior became increasingly disruptive, with many temper tantrums and physical outbursts. The Hartmanns argue that these problems were the result of Mark's frustration. Although Mark's behavior regressed through the school year, the Board removed Meagan Kelly from a supervisory role and stopped utilizing the services of outside consultants, until after Mark's IEP was changed to the self-contained program. The personnel changes and the cessation of supplementary consulting services by inclusion experts are key factors that convince the Court that the Board was no longer committed to Mark's inclusion. No autistic student had been fully included at Ashburn Elementary School before Mark. Mark was, in essence, a test case for Loudoun County. However, because there is abundant unequivocal evidence that other school systems have been able to educate Mark in the inclusive setting, the only conclusion is that the Board simply did not take enough appropriate steps to try to include Mark in a regular class.

2. Comparison of Educational Benefits

The Hearing Officer also found that the record did not establish that Mark received any educational benefit in an included setting and that Mark learns best when he is being taught in a one-to-one setting.

It is unclear to this Court how the Hearing Officer arrived at her conclusion that Mark did not learn anything while in an inclusive setting. Mark's disability significantly affects his ability to communicate. The record shows that Mark cannot be tested under standard conditions, yet the Hearing Officer appears to have discounted any evaluations based on adapted testing. This approach dooms Mark to constant failure.

The Hearing Officer notes that in assessing the educational benefit from regular education, the <u>Daniels R.R.</u> court looked at "the student's ability to grasp the essential elements of the regular education curriculum." At the second grade level the essential elements are basic math, reading and writing skills. Mark's teacher at Ashburn Elementary, Debra Jarrett, testified that she did not think Mark was learning in her class and she doubted Mark had the ability to do math or read.

However, Cathy Thornton, a tutor hired by the Hartmanns who worked with Mark after school during the 1993-94 school year, testified to the contrary. While tutoring Mark, Thornton was also employed by the Fairfax County public school system as a special education teacher for autistic students in a self-contained setting. Thornton made adaptations to standardized tests and was able to administer a portion of them to Mark. She concluded from this testing that Mark is not mentally retarded and is capable of making educational progress. She also testified that Mark does have the ability to do math and initiates social interactions. She observed that his attention span (lasted) from ten minutes to forty-five minutes when engaging in an academic activity.

Because Thornton appears to have no educational bias, the Court found her evidence to be especially credible and is perplexed by the Hearing Officer's failure to give this evidence due weight. (Note #4: The Hearing Officer also failed to give any weight to the previous education of Mark in an inclusion setting in Illinois.) She may well be the witness with the most hands-on experience educating autistic children. She testified to having eleven years of special education experience with at least one autistic child in her class each year. For the past five years she has taught in a Fairfax County autistic program in a self-contained classroom. (Tr. Sept. 28 at 141.) She obviously has an open mind about the most appropriate setting for autistic children. For example, she testified she believes one student in her class would benefit from an inclusion program while the rest of her students belonged in the self-contained setting. (<u>Id.</u> At 178.)

Kenna Colley, an inclusion specialist teacher who has been working with Mark at Kipps Elementary School in Montgomery County,

Virginia, corroborated Thornton's evaluation of Mark's potential. She testified that by the end of fourth grade Mark could independently do simple addition skills and was working on subtraction skills. Colley also testified that Mark engaged in social interaction with his classmates. He would bring things over to them in class, dance with them in music class and sled with them after school. Colley believed that Mark knew his classmates by name as evidenced by his properly pointing to a picture of a classmate when given a name and asked who the person was. Patrick Schwarz, an autism expert hired by the Hartmanns to observe Mark in his classroom, testified that based on his observations he determined that Mark had an attention span of approximately fifty minutes. Beverly Strager, Mark's fourth grade teacher at Kipps Elementary, testified at trial that Mark did make educational progress during the year in her regular education classroom. Similarly, Greg Paynter, Mark's fourth grade aide at Kipps Elementary, testified at trial that Mark made educational progress over the year and was able to work independently on adapted academic lessons by, for example, answering questions about a subject by selecting the proper answer from a word bank.

Besides the testimony of several Montgomery County, Virginia, educators concerning Mark's successful inclusion in their program, the Court also observed at trial videotape taken of Mark over a two-day period. That tape contains the best evidence of Mark's educational accomplishments because it shows Mark himself. For example, the Court saw Mark correctly point to a picture of Monticello out of a series of choices when asked for the home of Thomas Jefferson. He was able to point correctly to pictures of the appropriate coins when asked to give his aide 35 cents. As for Mark's behavior, outside of some cooing noises and limb movement, Mark exhibited no more disruptive behavior than his classmates did. There was no evidence of uncontrollable behavior. Mark learned to tolerate change better. For example, he was no longer afraid of the lunchroom, and was able to cope with calendar changes. He interacted better with peers and was sometimes seen to mimic smiles of classmates. He correctly labeled pictures of the school gym and playground.

The Board's witnesses tried to diminish the value of these accomplishments by essentially testifying to all the age appropriate things Mark does not appear to be doing. Although no witness claimed that Mark was working at his age level, as plaintiffs correctly argue, Mark is learning in the inclusive setting and he has more chance of fulfilling his unknown potential in such a setting than in the less enriched one of the self-contained class.

If Mark were placed in the self-contained autism class at Leesburg, he would be competing with five other autistic students for the attention of the special education teacher and the aide, he would not be exposed to a large number of verbal, normally social students whose behaviors he could pattern and he would not get the academic content he is presently receiving.

3. Effect on the Regular Classroom Environment

The Hearing Officer found that Mark engages in very disruptive behavior that has a negative effect on the environment in the classroom. She noted that while this factor standing alone would not be sufficient to justify removing Mark from the classroom, it weighs in with the other factors and contributed to her determination that it would be proper to remove Mark from the inclusion setting.

The record demonstrates that Mark had some behavioral problems at Ashburn Elementary. For example, Fred Jernigan was contacted by phone early on to suggest behavior modification strategies. However, Jernigan did not have any significant experience with teaching autistic children. When his credentials are compared with those of Thornton, Ruppmann, and Kelly it is obvious that he would be unable to come up with successful strategies. Although the problems continued, a behavior modification plan was not developed until February 1994. Cathy Thornton testified that she did not have problems with Mark's behavior during their tutoring sessions that year after school. Moreover, after Mark left Ashburn Elementary his behavior greatly improved. His Montgomery County, Virginia, fourth grade teacher, Beverly Strager, testified that Mark had a mild level of distractibility but never interfered with her teaching. She stated that when Mark made noises he would follow her instructions or the instructions of his classmates to quiet down. His aide, Greg Paynter, testified that Mark's behavior improved throughout that year, except during the period around the time when his mother became ill.

Given the strong presumption for inclusion under the IDEA, disruptive behavior should not be a significant factor in determining the appropriate educational placement for a disabled child. In Mark's case, there is strong evidence that his behaviors do not have a negative impact on his current environment. The videotape showed Mark engaging appropriately in many different activities: preparing for the day by taking the chairs off the desks, having lunch with his classmates, looking through a book with a classmate, working on the computer, raising his hand in response to a question by his teacher, and working one-to-one with his speech and language teacher. At no time did Mark's behavior become a disruption in the classroom. He seems to function as an integral member of the class. He also seems to take directions very well. In one instance Mark became tired and took a break by lying on the floor while working with his speech and language teacher. As soon as the teacher indicated that the break was over, Mark returned to his seat and resumed working. This evidence together with evidence that Mark has made educational progress in an included setting favors an included educational placement for Mark.

Considering that the efforts made by the Board to successfully accommodate Mark's placement decreased over the 1993-94 school year, this Court finds that Loudoun County Public Schools violated its obligation under the IDEA to educate Mark, to the maximum extent possible, with non-disabled children.

B. Appropriateness of the Proposed Placement

The Hearing Officer addressed the second issue regarding the appropriateness of the proposed placement after her determination that Loudoun County had not violated its duty under the IDEA. This Court having found a violation of the IDEA, need not address this issue but shall address it briefly for the sake of completeness.

The Board's proposed placement of Mark in a self-contained autism class would not be appropriate. The evidence demonstrates that Mark's greatest need is to improve his communications skills. The best environment for developing these skills is with children who communicate normally. Moreover, mainstreaming opportunities provided during the "specials," such as physical education, music, art and library classes, would not be appropriate for Mark. As Dr. Schwarz testified, these classes are less structured than core classes. Because Mark needs structure, he would not achieve the same improvements in his communication skills if the only mainstreaming opportunities provided were during unstructured and often chaotic classes.

Schwarz also testified that taking Mark out of his normal, included setting and placing him in the self-contained class would not be appropriate and be a setback. This is because in the self-contained classroom there are fewer routines, much less student initiation, and very limited interaction with age-appropriate peers. Kenna Colley testified that inclusion is very important for Mark if he is to learn skills necessary for his future. Such skills include how to stay on a task and engage in social interaction and certain academic skills. Colley believes that inclusion has been beneficial to Mark because his social skills have improved and his self-esteem has been heightened.

There was much discussion at trial about the skills important for Mark's future. Witnesses for the Board testified that Mark needs to focus on life skills including skills involving interaction in the community, such as going to the store or riding public transportation. There is unrefuted evidence that Mark is receiving such opportunities at home. Joseph Hartmann testified that he and his wife spend a lot of time teaching Mark about the community. Mark is often taken to the library, grocery store, bookstore and similar places. He was taught how to ride a bus. Further, Mark has been taught at home to complete tasks such as doing the dishes and taking out the garbage. Because Mark gets abundant training in life skills at home, this should not be the focus of his academic curriculum.

Conclusion

For the foregoing reasons, the Court REVERSES the decision of the Hearing Officer regarding the appropriate program and placement for Mark Hartmann. The Court finds that if the Board implemented its placement plan it would violate its duty under the IDEA to educate Mark, to the maximum extent appropriate, with children who are not disabled. The Court also finds that the Board's efforts to include Mark were inadequate because the Board failed to follow the advice of properly qualified experts like Ruppmann and Kelly, and instead placed staff on the IEP team who had inadequate training and experience, thereby dooming their inclusion efforts to failure. Therefore, judgment is entered in favor of plaintiffs and an appropriate Order will issue enjoining further violations of the IDEA and the Rehabilitation Act. Plaintiffs are awarded reasonable attorneys' fees and costs pursuant to 20 U.S.C. - 1415(4)(b), for both this matter and the administrative proceedings.

The Clerk is directed to forward copies of this Memorandum Opinion to counsel of record.

- Entered this 27th day of November, 1996.

In a written press release, Mr. Rugel wrote "Judge Brinkema's decision represented a complete victory for the Hartmanns." For the moment, we felt vindicated and victorious, that our voices were finally heard! Judge Binkema more justly took in to account the entirety of Mark's history, from Illinois to

Kipps E.S., whereas the hearing officer in the due process hearing failed to consider the full magnitude of Mark's success in the inclusive kindergarten/first-grade settings in Illinois. Given this, Judge Brinkema saw clear evidence to drive home her decision. In overturning the earlier opinion of the due process hearing officer, Judge Brinkema's judgment finally brought our case to justice!

While we wanted to celebrate, to experience the joy of it all, we remained subdued, nonetheless. Our energy was nearly exhausted—we were spent. We did celebrate the next day, however, with a prayer of thanks as we sat down for our family's Thanksgiving Day meal.

Any feelings of elation over Judge Brinkema's decision were short lived, however. On December 10, 1996, Ms. Mehfoud filed a Memorandum in Support of Motion for Stay in the Federal District Court in Alexandria. Just when we thought we'd finally won Mark's right to an inclusive education through LCPS, the legal battle began at the federal appellate court level.

CHAPTER 19

⑥

FOURTH CIRCUIT COURT OF APPEALS
July 8, 1997

LCPS's continuing efforts to bury us legally caught the attention of a wide spectrum of advocates within the disability and educational communities. Once LCPS appealed Judge Brinkema's decision to the Fourth Circuit Court of Appeals in Richmond, Virginia, we soon acquired a broad range of unsolicited support in the form of *amicus curiae* briefs, or "friends of the court" briefs. The Department of Education, the Department of Justice, and *sixteen other organizations* representing the varied interests of people with disabilities joined in preparing compelling briefs in support of Judge Brinkema's decision and our case in the fight for Mark's educational rights.

Notwithstanding, on May 9, 1997, the three-judge panel of the Fourth Circuit Court of Appeals took just over one hour to hear legal arguments from both Ms. Mehfoud and Mr. Rugel, and to question them on applicable case law. Unlike in Brinkema's courtroom, there were no witnesses called and no further evidence allowed at this level. Basically, the Fourth Circuit appellate court made its decisions based solely on the written record from the due process hearing and the Federal District Court's bench trial. Chief Judge J. Havie Wilkinson III, Circuit Judge Michael J. Luttig, and U.S. District Judge John Thomas Copenhaver, Jr. were designated to hear the appeal. Chief Judge Wilkinson wrote the decisive opinion in which Judge Luttig and Judge Copenhaver joined in *Hartmann v. Loudon County Board of Education,* 118 F.3d (4th Cir. Appeals 1997).

Early on, one of the judges made a comment that stung us deeply. He basically referred to Judge Brinkema as a "social worker," given the manner in which she wrote her decision. We viewed the comment as sarcastic, unprofessional, and disturbing—and feared that it forecast the overriding view of the Fourth Circuit in adjudicating LCPS's appeal.

At the time of the appeal, the political makeup of the Fourth Circuit judiciary was also quite interesting to note. The majority of the judges were conservatives, appointed by either President Ronald Reagan or President George H. Bush. Judge Brinkema was a relatively new federal judge appointed by President William J. Clinton. From our perspective, the disdain that the Fourth Circuit judges held for Judge Brinkema was palpable.

In the end and to our absolute dismay, on July 8, 1997, the Fourth Circuit Court of Appeals overturned Judge Brinkema's decision and upheld LCPS's position to place Mark in a self-contained special education setting.

The panel of judges wrote: "(The) lower court (i.e., Judge Brinkema) substituted its own notions of sound educational policy for those of the local school authorities and disregarded findings in the state's administrative proceedings. The IDEA does not require the furnishing of every special service necessary to maximize each handicapped child's potential."

According to the Fourth Circuit Court, evidence showed that when Mark made real progress in Illinois or in Montgomery County, it was in a one-on-one setting. The Fourth Circuit Court judged that weight should have been placed on where Mark made the most progress academically and that this outweighed his progress in social interactions.

Their decision was also based on the court's view that the training of Loudoun staff was not as bad as Judge Binkema had indicated. "To demand more than this from regular education personnel would essentially require them to become special education teachers trained in the full panoply of disabilities that their students might have. Virginia law does not require this, nor does the IDEA.... We can think of few steps that would do more to usurp state educational standards and policy than to have federal courts re-write state teaching certification requirements in the guise of applying the IDEA."

The Fourth Circuit Court also concluded that Mark's disruptive behavior was ignored by the lower court and was very relevant. Furthermore, it judged that Nancy McBride, the local hearing officer, did a painstaking job of getting to the facts of the case and that the lower court ignored her work.

To Continue the Legal Fight – or Not?

Following our grave disappointment with the decision of the Fourth Circuit Court of Appeals, Ms. Judith Heumann, Assistant Secretary for Special Education and Rehabilitation within the U.S. Department of Education, invited Roxana, Mr. Rugel, and Ms. Ruppmann to her office to discuss the legal strategies open to us at this juncture. In attendance at that round-table discussion were lawyers from the Department of Education as well as the Department of Justice. After nearly two hours of deliberation, the consensus was that we should proceed to the Supreme Court with our case; there was everything to gain and nothing to lose.

We therefore drafted and filed a Petition for a Writ of Certiorari with the United States Supreme Court in Washington, D.C. A Petition for a Writ of Certiorari is a formal request of the Supreme Court to hear a case. Few cases meet the criteria established for the Court to hear legal arguments. However, Mr. Rugel hoped that our case, focused on the education of children with disabilities with implications for the entire country, would meet the measure. This was our last hope for justice. LCPS also filed a Conditional Petition for a Writ of Certiorari in case the Supreme Court agreed to hear our case.

Within weeks of receiving our petition, the Supreme Court exercised its prerogative *not* to hear the case. The legal battle was over. We had exhausted every possible option available within the judicial system.

While we were ultimately not successful in the legal struggle with LCPS, our fight for Mark's inclusive education focused the nation for a span of five years on the plight of children with disabilities, special education practices, and the Individuals with Disabilities Education Act. Throughout the legal process, we took measures to keep Mark fully included and in safe hands in Blacksburg, Virginia. Through it all, we remained convinced by the clear evidence showing that our son benefitted from a fully included public education and worsened when removed from that powerful learning environment. Therefore, following the legal loss to Loudoun County Public Schools, we ultimately chose to keep Mark enrolled in Montgomery County Public Schools, in Blacksburg, Virginia, throughout the remainder of his school years.

AFTERWORD

MARK'S SENIOR YEAR
2004 and Beyond

Something was amiss. Roxana noticed that Mark didn't relish dinner as normal for her eighteen-year-old son, and he was rather subdued. He didn't show his usual interest in watching videotapes either, but rather, chose to lie in bed reading a magazine about large jungle cats. On that cold and gloomy February night in 2004, Mark Hartmann sprung up from his bed and approached his mother with urgency where she sat in the next room at her desktop computer. He motioned that he wanted to sit down by gently pushing Roxana to the side—she moved at his touch.

"Don't feel good, hurt," Mark typed on the computer. Roxana verbally asked Mark if his stomach was hurting. Agitated, Mark typed, "No, no. Stomach feels good." Roxana looked directly into Mark's eyes and implored, "Mark, tell me where you hurt." At once, Mark turned to the computer keyboard and typed, "Yes, ear." Roxana then repeated to Mark her understanding of what he had written, that his ear was hurting him. Mark responded, "Yes, yes." Roxana asked, "Which ear, Mark?" and Mark immediately placed his hand over his right ear. *Could he have swimmer's ear?* Roxana wondered. Mark's routine did include an hour of swimming laps at the recreation center after school, each day.

At once, Roxana took Mark to the emergency room. The doctor examined him and confirmed that, indeed, Mark had an infected right ear. After stopping to pick up the prescribed antibiotic, Roxana brought Mark back home, relieved. She praised him for taking the initiative to tell her about his ear. Roxana was overjoyed that Mark had typed his thoughts for her— totally independently!

High School Years

During the school year 2003-2004, Mark was a senior at Blacksburg High

School. Throughout his life as a student, Mark's autism has impacted the normal development of his communication and social skills. Being totally non-verbal, Mark relied on body language and his computer to make his thoughts known to others. At school, Mark communicated by independently using a communication board and by using facilitated communication (FC) on his laptop computer, receiving facilitation support from trained staff closest to him. Since the primary goal for Mark's education had always been for him to achieve independent communication, Mark tried and successfully used many different augmentative communication methods over the years, including FC. These methods all contributed to the development of Mark's communication abilities and increased his confidence in using those skills.

Mid-way through his sophomore year, Mark became impatient with facilitated communication and began typing single words and familiar phrases on his own, sometimes repeatedly. Recognizing that he was testing his own ability and becoming more independent with typing, Mark's teachers began fading their level of FC support.

Well into his senior year, we were overjoyed when Mark arrived at a critical communication threshold—Mark no longer required a facilitator to help him express himself in writing! Mark was, finally, able to type sentences independently within the school environment, especially in response to questions about his academic classes. Mark could even compose a term paper on a given topic—although it was painstakingly difficult and required a much longer completion time for him, compared to the average senior. However, it became obvious to us over time that Mark was much more comfortable communicating facts as he'd learned them from books/computer assignments, rather than using his independent communication skills to be social. Such communication limitations are typical in individuals with autism and underscore the devastating effect that autism has on a person's abilities for spontaneous social interaction.

Behaviorally, in his relatively short life, Mark has learned to control multiple, unwanted behaviors associated with his autism. Along the way, he has developed into a charming young man able to cope with life within the standard social norms expected of older teenagers. Nonetheless, there is always a slight chance that an unexpected event, such as a fire alarm, will cause Mark great personal stress. If he judges he can't handle the circumstances, Mark will now let us know. We try to help him cope during the event if an easy exit is not available. Similarly, in high school, Mark's teachers were all aware of the telltale signs that he was beginning to lose control. On those rare occasions, they reacted according to the Positive Behavior Support Plan in place and simply moved Mark to a quiet place where he could relax and regain his composure.

Despite such gains, autism continues to deny Mark the reasoning abilities needed to assess potential harm in circumstances or to analyze how to avoid accidents. Throughout his educational experience, Mark required an assistant to guide him at school and in the community, primarily to keep him safe from harm. Similarly, and even though he has been coached for years about being careful when crossing the street, we still walk close to Mark in order to grab him should he forget to "look both ways before crossing."

Regular physical activity continues to help Mark stay focused, avoid repetitive and stimulatory behavior, and get a good night's sleep. We believe that these physical activities have also been instrumental in keeping Mark totally free from pharmaceuticals throughout his life. Mark's regular activities include swimming, basketball, power walks, bike rides, and visits to larger retail stores that have book/video sections. On a near daily basis, he swims laps for an hour or so before taking his turn in the whirlpool. After a hot shower, Mark is totally relaxed, in a fabulous mood, and ready for whatever comes next on his evening agenda. On weekends, in addition to swimming, walks, basketball, and attending Mass at St. Mary's Catholic Church, Mark also enjoys going to the movies. He especially enjoys animated adventure films, but is also interested in PG action movies.

During the school year, Mark worked two jobs arranged by the special education Community Instruction (CI) staff at Blacksburg High School. This "job sampling" was designed to expose Mark to the world of commerce and to teach him the discipline required to complete assigned tasks in a work environment. On Wednesdays after school, Mark worked for approximately two hours at the office complex of the President of Virginia Tech. There, he distributed interoffice mail, collected/shredded discarded sensitive papers, and photocopied official notices for the secretaries, as required. Mark was proud to have had his own office and his name listed on the building directory. Then, on Saturday afternoons, Mark worked at a local retail store restocking products on store shelves. Depending on the products requiring restock, he worked up to three hours each shift with five-minute breaks every half-hour.

During the summer months, in addition to continuing his job at Virginia Tech, Mark had a daily job at a large grocery store chain. He was responsible for retrieving shopping carts from the parking lot, dry mopping the store's aisles, stocking shelves (mostly the larger-sized items for proprioceptive sensory needs), and running the box-crusher machine. His job at the grocery store rarely exceeded the two hours scheduled for that activity, demonstrating that Mark was able to successfully accomplish job demands within allotted time frames.

Simply put, Mark loved his jobs! Though the process of introducing Mark to the workplace was deliberately slow, once he understood job expectations, he had no problem accomplishing assigned tasks. He always looked forward to going to work and walked with pride, especially while wearing his employee-uniform shirt at the grocery store. Furthermore, the people Mark worked with were all supportive of the ultimate goal: to give Mark a positive work experience and thereby boost his self-confidence.

Even though Mark attended school with the same group of children since third grade, he had only a few close friends who provided regular socialization opportunities during the school day and at school events. These girls and boys had hearts of gold and understood that their friendship with Mark was a one-way street: because of his autism, Mark simply could not express his thoughts or respond normally during social interactions. Because of his autism, Mark was not capable of acknowledging his friends or even saying "thank you," except in very subtle ways: his soft touch on their cheek, a wave of his hand. Sharing "high fives" served as a way for Mark and his classmates to congratulate and greet one another throughout the school day. Through such subtle signs, it was clear to teachers and to us that Mark really enjoyed being included in and treated as one of the group.

Other high school classmates were equally sensitive to Mark's peculiarities and to his needs. Through peer training over the years, they learned to accommodate Mark in the classroom and to be patient with him. They also learned to assess Mark's disposition and determine whether or not he was becoming anxious. Several classmates even volunteered to learn facilitated communication techniques in order to help Mark express himself. While everyone welcomed their initiative, developing the touch and familiarity required to be an effective FC-facilitator takes considerable time, training and practice. In spite of their willingness to learn, schoolmates never quite passed the rudimentary learning stages in communicating with Mark via FC techniques.

Beyond school, Mark has begun to advocate for other children with disabilities. Today, he is a self-advocate who has a great sense of humor and enjoys sharing his success in education at conferences focused on autism and/or inclusion. Mark and another young man with autism were invited to serve as guest presenters at a conference on Autism Spectrum Disorders in Roanoke, Virginia, where they presented on the topic of Facilitated Communication. While edgy at first, within minutes of sitting behind the table on stage, Mark became serious and focused. For forty-five minutes, Mark listened to questions from parents and educators, offering his typewritten responses which were then projected onto a large, overhead screen in the meeting hall.

At one point during the presentation, the other young man with autism began to lose his composure and could not immediately continue. A slight commotion erupted. Without being prompted, Mark independently wrote,

"Yes. Matt, you just have to relax and have some fun." This certainly conveyed Mark's solution for handling the stress of the moment!

During that conference, Mark's facilitator helped extinguish fires of doubt over FC by demonstrating fading techniques that can be practiced to help the person being facilitated reach total independence. Indeed, Mark has become more and more comfortable with independent typing on the computer. While his need for support from a facilitator has lessened dramatically, and while *capable* of communicating totally on his own using his laptop computer, Mark's independent communication is usually limited to brief conversations. Much of Mark's communicative ability depends upon his anxiety level, the urgency of the message being communicated, and his mood. In general, Mark communicates especially well when he is relaxed and in good spirits. Although he has come far, he has not yet broken through that invisible ceiling that would allow consistent, reliable independence in his attempts to communicate.

Elements of Successful Inclusion

Mark's successful inclusion at Blacksburg High School was founded on elements established early on during his education, possibly going as far back as kindergarten. While not perfect, the communication systems used at school served the inclusion team well and ensured that Mark learned the material being taught. Mark proved himself to be an active thinker who enjoyed learning class material. A near-perfectionist due to his autism, Mark did not like when he got a question wrong on a test, but he learned to live with it. Over the years, Mark learned to be comfortable with the structure and routine of school. He gradually learned coping skills to help override the anxiety he felt by having someone work closely with him.

We believe that the cornerstone of Mark's success, however, was the transition between middle and high schools. We joined with administrators, teachers, and therapists to form a strong team committed to making Mark's high school inclusion program successful. That team formulated excellent plans and best strategies to develop support structures for Mark and appropriate accommodations for him at school. (Note: Early in Mark's education, we used as many as 35 separate accommodations to ensure success in Mark's inclusion. By his senior year, those accommodations had shrunk to only five. Full accommodations are key to a successful inclusion program.)

Mark's educational plan was characterized by six key elements: consistency at school; a definitive daily structure; effective transition planning; teacher/peer training; an effective positive behavioral support plan; and a team of committed, willing, educational professionals. We believe that these elements were so significant to Mark's successful inclusion, they bear additional comment here:

Consistency: Montgomery Country Public Schools hired Mr. Daniel Ferrell, Mark's eighth grade teacher's aide, as a high school Special Education teacher. Mr. Ferrell had completed a Master's Degree in Special Education and was eager to work at the high school level. Coming with Mark from middle school, Mr. Ferrell remained Mark's special education teacher throughout his high school years. Knowing Mark especially well and understanding the importance of structure in Mark's life, Mr. Ferrell also provided the key to effective staff training and the consistent implementation of Mark's Individual Education Plan (IEP).

In addition, Mr. Ferrell and the school's speech therapist, Mrs. Terry Robinson, excelled in using FC to help Mark communicate in the classroom and to complete homework assignments. Through training provided by Montgomery County Public Schools, they became knowledgeable of the FC process designed to help Mark achieve fully independent communication. After years of facilitation, Mark has reached a high level of expressive fluency and has moved closer and closer to independence.

While the teacher's aides at school were not as advanced in facilitating with Mark as Mr. Ferrell and Mrs. Robinson, nonetheless, they were successful intermediaries for him. The aides helped keep Mark on track with his studies, paid attention to indicators that he was becoming restless, and monitored his yes/no/multiple-choice answers on quizzes.

As the person overall responsible for Mark's high school education, Mr. Ferrell carefully screened, trained, monitored, and advised the teacher's aides hired to accompany Mark throughout his school day. Mr. Ferrell keenly watched Mark's demeanor for any signs indicating that a problem was brewing. In many instances, Mark's anxiety was related to the calendar or an upcoming event, such as a family member's birthday, a school dance, or an upcoming holiday. Together, Mr. Ferrell and Mark would discuss Mark's concerns and resolve them as quickly as possible through adaptation/accommodation. New special education teachers would have needed months each year to learn Mark's particular foibles and to develop strategies to accommodate them. Thus, the consistent supervision and management provided by MCPS through Mr. Ferrell's oversight proved invaluable to Mark's overall success.

Structure: After several difficult weeks adjusting to the change in routine from middle school to high school, Mr. Ferrell and the collective special education staff realized that Mark needed more time to mentally prepare for school work in the formal classroom. Mark appeared stressed by the long hours in class. The staff, therefore, recommended that Mark's class load be reduced from five substantive subjects to four. Within days of the change, Mark demonstrated noticeable improvements in his anxiety level and his ability to attend to schoolwork.

Maintaining four classes plus physical education and two study halls worked well for Mark throughout his freshman/sophomore years. This schedule allowed him time to complete class assignments at school and was flexible enough for Mark to relax between classes, if needing a break. Mark earned a "B-"grade average for his first two years of high school. His junior and senior years, Mark again took four subjects but no longer needed to take PE, thereby freeing up another study period. Near the end of high school, Mark had a straight "A" average for the year!

Because he carried a reduced course load each year, we knew it would take Mark at least a fifth—or perhaps even a sixth—year of schoolwork to earn his regular academic high school diploma. Nonetheless, since Mark truly enjoyed the routine of high school, the extra time in class was not a hardship for him. He enrolled in a freshman-level English Composition course at Virginia Tech University in Blacksburg to earn the last of his required high school credits. This arrangement, established by MCPS and the executive officers at Virginia Tech, resulted in the creation of the On Campus Transition Program (OCTP), now serving seven young adults in Blacksburg. Through this structured program, Mark spent about four hours a day at Virginia Tech—in class, studying at the library, having lunch on campus, and using the athletic facilities. He particularly enjoyed the occasional encounter with classmates from high school who were also students at the university.

Transition Planning: During seventh grade, we first participated in a process known as MAP or "Making an Action Plan," along with Mark, selected teachers, peers, family members, and friends. The MAP mandrel focuses on Mark as a person, defining who Mark is, his dreams and worst nightmares, his talents and strengths. MAP sets forth a general action plan to help Mark avoid those nightmares and make his dreams come true. As a young man with ideas of his own, Mark always participated in the MAP round-table discussions, expressing his dreams, fears, likes, and dislikes.

During the winter of his freshman year in high school, Mark's MAP group met again to plan for the next steps in Mark's life journey. Using the outline provided by the MAP process, the group laid out a "PATH" for Mark, called the "Planning Alternative – Tomorrow with Hope." Again, Mark participated in the discussions. The PATH produced a collage of ideas and goals for Mark, which laid out an action plan and strategies for Mark to realize his dreams, both near and far. It included a concrete vision and timetable for reaching goals through the end of his sophomore year. For example, one goal on Mark's PATH concerned "travel by air on vacation." We were tasked with assisting Mark in accomplishing this goal, so in late-January 2003—over a four-day weekend—we arranged for Mark to vacation in the Bahamas to enjoy the sun, the beach, swimming in the ocean, relaxing, and drinking ice-cold Sprite, his favorite soft drink. Not only did Mark love the experience, but it seemed to boost his self-confidence regarding his ability to cope with the maze of security measures and long airport waits. More importantly, Mark is now more comfortable with air travel and the changes in settings/people that accompany that reality. Planning for Mark's future and related transitions has given us a framework to chart the next phase of Mark's life and to help him achieve his own personal goals and dreams.

Training of Teachers and Peers: While inclusion programs may vary, all educators agree that inclusion must be planned out based on each child's needs as an individual. For Mark, the special education staff at Blacksburg High School, as well as the administrators of Montgomery County Public Schools, performed exceptionally well in managing Mark's inclusion program. These educational professionals were well trained and carried an undying commitment to building Mark's success, one day at a time.

It takes considerable patience and concerted effort for school districts to educate classroom teachers about inclusive education. There is more to a successful inclusion program than initially meets the eye. The various licenses and endorsements brought by teachers to their profession are only the beginning of their education, when it comes to inclusion. Provisions have to be made for teachers to attend conferences/courses to equip them with strategies to successfully implement an inclusion program for children with disabilities. Furthermore, these efforts must be on-going, year after year, in order to develop teachers/staff capable of finding solutions for and overcoming the challenges related to inclusion. Their success, in the end, benefits not only the children with disabilities, but all of the children in the classroom.

Beginning with the fourth grade and each year thereafter, Roxana joined the school's special education staff during the first weeks of school to conduct peer training for Mark's classmates that year. Because of anxiety felt when discussions centered on him, Mark was not present during these peer-training sessions. During the scheduled class periods, Mark was introduced to the class *as a person*. Roxana and staff talked about his disability and described the dos/don'ts for successful interactions with Mark. The teachers joined Roxana in addressing the children's questions and concerns during open discussions following each presentation. The children in school with Mark in prior years also loved sharing their own experiences. These sessions considerably enhanced his classmates' abilities to welcome Mark as a member of the class throughout the remainder of the year.

Positive Behavioral Support: From his earliest days in school, the various education teams working with Mark always provided teachers with a guide explaining how to best handle his unwanted behaviors. On a positive note, this informal behavioral support guide never employed the approaches used most commonly in segregated special education programs, such as aversives, physical restraints, and/or behavior modification techniques. Yet while this informal how-to guide worked well for staff/teachers and was passed on from year to year, it fell short of actually "managing" Mark's behaviors.

Beginning in sixth grade, however, a more structured strategy was used, called the Positive Behavior Support Plan (PBSP). Over time and with data that recorded the circumstances of the behaviors themselves, the PBSP emerged. Realizing that atypical social skills and communication challenges (both characteristic of autism) were at the root of Mark's unwanted behaviors, the PBSP basically provided a formula for mitigating unwanted behaviors. It clearly defined the problem; presented a hypothesis regarding the problem behavior; identified the communication, social, or other skills needing to be taught/reinforced to reduce the problem behavior; and outlined antecedent strategies that were required to avoid it. Additionally, the PBSP included a hierarchy of consequential strategies to use when the behavior occurred.

Recognizing that, in some instances, the identified problem behavior could escalate to a crisis situation, a specific crisis plan was clearly established as part of the PBSP. The crisis intervention plan thereby ensured that a worst-case scenario would be addressed with a measured, effective response.

The PBSP used at Blacksburg High School provided staff with guidance concerning Mark's behavioral data and set a schedule for formally reviewing/ evaluating that data. In sum, Blacksburg's PBSP was a *living document* and part of the IEP, which was modified as needed to accommodate Mark's individualized needs. Use of such a consistent, structured, well-intentioned plan was the key to near problem-free behavior for Mark throughout high school!

A Committed Team of Educational Professionals: While the special education teacher and speech therapist were previously lauded for their work with Mark at Blacksburg High School, it takes more than a teacher or two to establish a winning inclusion program. Thanks to the excellence of the special education administrators in the central office and at Blacksburg High School, the leadership of the principal, and the constancy of the entire teaching staff, Mark's inclusion program proceeded apace for four years with hardly a missed beat. There was a real cooperative, compassionate spirit that pervaded nearly all the teachers and a majority of the students at Blacksburg High, positively affecting how they related to children with disabilities. It is fair to say that inclusion had a direct impact on the high school—all for the better, for each and every child. In this way, it was a win-win situation for everyone!

Plans for the Future

While we have a vision for Mark's future, remaining flexible is at the core of our thoughts as we consider life for him beyond high school and for when he is no longer under parental care. There are a variety of community-based options open to him.

Through the PATH process, certain goals have been established for Mark's immediate and long-term future. Concerning college, everyone working with Mark at home and at school clearly understands that he must achieve consistent, independent communication in order to continue his college education toward a bachelor's degree. Without it, Mark's school days as a part-time college student will likely be over. At the same time, however, we see value in enrolling Mark in select college and perhaps internet-based courses simply to stimulate his intellectual growth during the planned, structured activities that will form Mark's future daily routine.

Ideally, Mark will live independently with a group of two to three college-aged young men, but nonetheless have a separate support structure in place to safeguard and guide him during his daily routine. With the support of a job coach, we anticipate that Mark will have a part-time job that earns him a monthly salary. He will remain physically active, especially concerning his daily swimming workouts. Mark will be able to take trips to visit family and friends, as well as go on vacation. Additionally, given the importance of the Catholic faith in his life, we suspect that Mark will want to continue attending Mass, both for spiritual renewal as well as the social benefits associated with belonging to Christ's family at church. In sum, we will strive to assist Mark in achieving a well-rounded lifestyle that includes a variety of meaningful activities that are personally rewarding and enjoyable for him. As parents, we only want Mark to be able to relax and have some fun—to enjoy life, and to have his needs and aspirations realized.

Mark's Insight

To conclude, we'd like to share a glimpse into autism as provided by Mark, himself. In response to an English composition assignment on April 19, 2001, Mark wrote:

Autism has been one aspect [of my life] that has made my journey very difficult. Autism has given me many difficulties to deal with. It has shaped the way I act, the way I see the world and begin each day. This journey of my life will be one with many challenges that must be overcome on so many levels – because they are very ingrained in who I am and the ways in which I behave.

The road I am traveling on was made especially for me by God, and therefore, I must do my best to be the best I can. This road is long and difficult—so the ones who are helping me along the way are much respected and loved by me. I know that together we can all overcome the problems that I face and strive to overcome.

Despite the problems arising from his autism, the challenges imposed by LCPS, and the loss of our legal battle—Mark has achieved remarkable success over the years! Mark successfully obtained his special education IEP diploma in 2004, but didn't stop there. Given his own hard work and the unwavering perseverance of family and a band of devoted educational professionals, Mark then went on to complete all the requirements for a *regular academic* high school diploma, including two credits earned while in the Transition Program at Virginia Tech University! Graduating from high school in 2007 with a *full academic diploma*, Mark Hartmann remained *fully included* with his non-disabled peers, victorious in the end!

Others join us, regularly, in recognizing that our son has grown into a remarkable young man. As a bright, capable, successful person with autism and not simply an "autistic person," there is so much more to Mark than just his disability. With appropriate supports, we are confident that he will continue to make on-going strides in the years to come.

As this story demonstrates, dedicated teachers, educational professionals, devoted family members, and friends can assist young people like Mark in realizing their aspirations, despite the very real challenges associated with autism. Indeed, Mark said it correctly, "Together we can all overcome the problems that I face and strive to overcome." And as Roxana once said, "This is not about winners and losers; this is about schools (and families and communities) doing the right thing for children." Whether you are the parent of a child with autism, an educator, legislator, family member, classmate, medical professional, or neighbor…we certainly invite you to do the right thing and make that difference!

APPENDIX

NEWS ANALYSIS

A feature article focused on Mark and the issue of inclusive education appeared in the October 17, 1994 edition of *People* magazine. The *Loudoun Times-Mirror* and the *Leesburg Today* newspapers maintained coverage of the case for nearly five years. The *Washington Post, Washington Hispanic, New York Times* and *USA Today* also covered the story as significant developments unfolded. We also made appearances on *This Morning*, on the *Today Show*, and on the *News Hour* to discuss the case and Mark's inclusion in a regular school classroom.

In 2001, Mr. Bruce Dorries of the Communications Department at Mary Baldwin College in Staunton, Virginia and Ms. Beth Haller of the Department of Mass Communication at Towson University, Towson, Maryland compiled articles, television tapes, and radio recordings of the extensive media coverage of our legal battle. They analyzed the narrative themes that each side of the inclusion issue used to support their arguments. Mr. Dorries and Ms. Haller published their analysis in the periodical, *Disability and Society* 16, no. 6 (2001): 871-891. The following excerpts are taken from that article:

> Inclusive education for disabled children has been a major focus for disability activists and parents of disabled children since the Individuals with Disabilities Education Act (IDEA) became law in 1975. Although a prominent topic in the minds of Americans with school-age children, the issue has only recently begun to attract media attention. News coverage of educational issues in general has improved over the years, and with that has come more attention to high-profile cases of inclusive education.
>
> One explanation for the current news media interest in inclusive education is that 20 years after it was first passed, IDEA was updated and re-authorized in 1997. The result of IDEA has been taking disabled children out of institutions and segregated special education

settings and integrating them into regular classrooms and school activities. The U.S. Department of Education reports that before IDEA, 90% of children with developmental disabilities received an education in state institutions (U.S. Department of Education, 2000). The Department of Education says that due to inclusive education programs today, three times the number of people with disabilities attend college and double the number of 20-year-olds with disabilities are working, when compared to pre-IDEA figures.

Inclusive education is nonetheless controversial. When it was only acceptable for children with minor learning disabilities, such as slight hearing impairments, the issue was less controversial. Notwithstanding, parents of non-disabled children have long been concerned that children with more severe disabilities, such as autism, can be disruptive to their child's education. Others worry about finite educational resources, if large amounts may be needed for severely disabled children. Studies show that although approximately one-third of children in the United States with special education needs receive an education in standard classrooms, few of these children have severe disabilities (Pae, 1994). The controversy has grown as severely disabled children and their families fight for inclusive education.

One high-profile case rocketed the topic of inclusive education to the national media attention in the mid-1990s. Beginning in 1995, *Hartmann v. Loudoun County Board of Education* tested whether or not schools must include severely disabled children in regular classrooms. Because of their long legal battle in Northern Virginia, the Hartmanns and the inclusion movement became almost synonymous. Mark Hartmann, who is autistic, became a symbol in a national debate over whether, and how often, disabled youngsters should be educated alongside their non-disabled peers (Wilgoren & Pae, 1994).

After providing a summary of the events that led to the dispute over Mark's education, Mr. Dorries and Ms. Haller analyzed the media coverage of the legal issues pertinent to the case:

Within the ritual view of communication (Carey, 1989), news stories are seen as culturally constructed narratives. Within this framework, news still has the power to inform, but Bird & Dardenne (1988) explain that the information audiences receive is not facts and figures, but a larger symbolic system of news narratives. As a method of communication, news can take on qualities like the myth. Both convey culture. News stories, like myths, do not "tell it like it is," but rather, "tell it like it means." In this study, news illustrates cultural narratives about inclusive education. Themes were embedded in the stories told by the actors in this social drama. The process of identifying narrative themes began after more than 90 news stories, editorials, commentaries, letters to the editor and three radio transcripts about the case were gathered and analyzed.

The themes are divided into those that support the Hartmanns or inclusion, and those that support the Loudoun County School District or are against inclusion (four narrative themes each). This division over-simplifies the nature of the public discussion about inclusion; there are more than two sides to this complex issue. Nonetheless, this division provides a more concrete, linear way to discuss the narratives and themes.

The themes found in narratives told by the Hartmanns and inclusion supporters include:

Theme 1: Everyone Wins with Inclusive Education

This narrative connects to an overarching theme imbedded within the IDEA legislation – that inclusive education benefits disabled children in the short run with better learning and, in the long run, with more employment and post-secondary educational opportunities. The benefit of inclusive education for non-disabled children is the ability to understand and cope with a more diverse society and people who are different from them. For example, a *New York Times* analysis piece on inclusive education embraces the narrative of IDEA that it benefits all children, not just those with disabilities. Many educators and parents believe that segregating children with disabilities is bad, both educationally and morally. They say such a policy undermines the development of both disabled children, by failing to give them a chance to develop the skills and relationships that they will need as adults, and other children, by preventing beneficial contact with the full range of people in their communities (Lewin, 1997, p. 20).

Mark Hartmann's mother, Roxana, most often provides this "everyone wins" narrative in both her quotes to media and her *Roanoke Times* commentary on her son's case. In the following narrative from her commentary, she explains the benefits of inclusive education for all children: "(Mark) has demonstrated that there are no long-term harmful effects on the classmates of a disabled child. In fact, full inclusion gives them an opportunity to embrace diversity and grow in compassion and understanding—honorable goals that will serve our children well through their lifetime. In sum, through inclusion, we can make our communities a better place for people with disabilities, one child and one family at a time, if we work together. It's the best thing to do for our future together" (Hartmann, 1998, A7).

The news media also relied on prominent pro-inclusion sources, which made the narrative compelling. In articles about the broader inclusive education topic, such as the following *New York Times* article, Judith Heumann, an assistant secretary in the Office of Special Education and Rehabilitative Services at the U.S. Department of Education, who is herself a wheelchair user, explains the "everyone wins" narrative in a national community context:

"Education is academic, but it's also social, learning how to live in a community, learning about differences," she said. "I tell parents who are afraid to send a child with disabilities into a regular setting that overprotection does no service when that disabled child becomes an adult. If your child was out of sight, out of mind, that doesn't change. People who might have become their friends in school won't know them." Academically, too, she said, all children can benefit from inclusion. "The methods that teachers learn from working with the disabled and individualizing instruction, are useful with other students, as well," Ms. Heumann said. "In a way, you can see every child as having special needs. So the ideal is a system in which every child gets an individualized education" (Lewin, 1997, p. 20).

The narrative takes on even more strength when adults with disabilities, who were the product of inclusive education, enter the discourse.

Theme 2: Inclusion is Cheaper

This narrative appears in two ways. One implied theme is that society benefits in general from inclusive education because well-educated disabled children mean future contributing, tax-paying members of society, rather than tax burdens. However, typically, the narrative was more overt: inclusive education costs less than institutionalization of severely disabled children.

Roxana Hartmann makes the argument that institutionalization is expensive and has long-term costs for society. "But the commonwealth does support large institutions. A large chunk of your tax dollars are spent in institutions. It costs more than $80,000 per year to support a person in an institution, and it's getting more expensive all the time. By the year 2000, the national average will reach $113,000 per person in an institution. There are 189,000 Virginians with mental retardation alone—the greater majority housed in institutions. But why is this relevant to the education of a disabled child? We know from experiences of our sister states that it all begins with decisions focused on educating the disabled child. Early intervention strategies and an inclusive education posture are proven as an effective approach to integrate our disabled citizens into the community with jobs that they can be trained for and normal home settings to live in. Community-based living and care works better than institutions and costs far less" (Hartmann, 1998, A7).

The message from the U.S. Department of Education about IDEA is similar. It estimates that educating students in neighborhoods, who would previously have been institutionalized, saves $10,000 per child (U.S. Department of Education, 2000). Consistent with notions of American pragmatism, this narrative ties to capitalistic notions of "the bottom line" in which citizens embrace policies that reduce taxes or give the most benefit for the least amount of tax dollars.

Theme 3: Human Rights Should Apply to Everyone in a Civilized Society

Typically, this narrative is tied to every American's right to a free public education. The right to an education is presented as a human right available to all equally.

Roxana Hartmann puts it succinctly. "After contemplating this response, I have decided to review some facts that may be overshadowed by accusations (real or imagined) and that may not be obvious to a casual observer. First of all, public education is the right of all children. The Individuals with Disabilities Act guarantees access for disabled students into the 'least restrictive environment.' The only measure is that the school must demonstrate that the disabled child is able to learn in the LRE with appropriate support, services and accommodations.

"...In all our debate, we should remember that each and every child in our community, including the disabled, is a valued human being who has a basic right to opportunity — whether we are talking work, education, housing or access to public buildings. To consider it otherwise will take us back to the 1860s" (Hartmann, 1998, p. A7).

Several members of the local Southwestern Virginia community continue the free and public education narrative in a number of letters to *The Roanoke Times*: "How does Professor Holladay justify (himself) saying that his daughter has more of a right to an education than my brother? Holladay is concerned about students who 'can learn algebra and Spanish, children for whom the schools are intended, and whose futures will depend on what they learn now.' All children's futures are determined by what they learn. This is a public school system and everyone has a right to an education" (Greenberg, 1998, p. A7). "Our community has chosen (inclusion) for more than 10 years, with all its pitfalls, challenges and magic, because we care about children. All children have a future, and in America, schools are intended for everyone" (Bickley & Bickley, 1998, p. A7). "Public schools aren't for the learning elite. They are public schools, and by law, must provide an appropriate education in the 'least restrictive environment' for all children. There is no such thing as separate but equal" (Eaton, 1998, A7).

Although an explicit link is not made, the theme within these statements is reminiscent of the education reforms that African Americans fought for in the 1950s and 1960s to bring about integrated public education for black and white children. The inclusion movement puts forth the same notion, separate but equal does not fit with American ideals.

Theme 4: Inclusive Education has Proven Itself

Specifically, this narrative tied into Mark Hartmann's success in an inclusive education environment before moving to Virginia and, broadly, the success of such programs nationally and in Blacksburg, Virginia where Mark Hartmann was placed early in the case. For example, Jamie Ruppmann, an education consultant who works with disabled children, saw Mark's success back in Illinois destroying the case of Loudoun County. Educators from Illinois did testify that Mark was successful in their inclusion program before the family moved to Virginia (DeVaughn, 1995a). As Roxana Hartmann explained: "All you have to know about this case is that Mark was successfully included in Illinois and in Montgomery County. The only place he could not be successfully included was Loudoun County, and that's clearly because the school system did not have the commitment to do it" (Benning, 1997b).

Hartmann continued this argument by explaining why she chose to move to Montgomery County: "[That county] is one of the few school districts in Virginia to honor and abide by IDEA—the law. Among other states, Virginia is ranked forty-sixth in its support of people with disabilities and their families" (Hartmann, 1998, p. A7).

Others made similar arguments. "I have heard nothing negative about having this child stay," the President of the Montgomery County Council of PTAs said. "What I have heard is: Why did the school system take a negative stand against this child in the first place? From a parent standpoint, this woman did everything she could for her kid (in Loudoun County), then set out to find what she could for him somewhere else".... "We need to show that it works so other school systems can try to do the same thing" (DeVaughn, 1995b, p. A1).

The successful inclusive education program narrative is also connected specifically to Mark's educational growth. Roxana Hartmann says: "He has blossomed in a very nurturing environment here with people who are dedicated and understand him and his disability. He'll stay here until he finishes school" (Lu, 1998, p. A1).

The Timmy Clemens case also bolsters the narrative of inclusive education "proving itself": Four years ago, Timmy Clemens could not walk near a classroom without becoming so scared he couldn't enter the room. His autism required a full-time aide and much patient coaxing to get him through a day. By his senior year last year, Timmy could walk to classes in Blacksburg High School on his own. With the help of his aide, Marc Eaton, and a special board that lists the alphabet and short words such as "yes" and "no", he did homework and took tests in courses such as algebra and honors history. Today, as a postgraduate, he works with an aide in a job at Blacksburg's Municipal Building. "Some truly believe in it; some think it's a waste," said Judy Clemens, Timmy's mother. "But other people's opinions don't matter," she said, because she can see the improvements in her son. "I don't think inclusion is perfect. But I think it's going to get better and better, and I'm proud of Montgomery County" (Applegate & Lu, 1998, p. A1).

Although these narrative themes in the Hartmann case advanced the cause of inclusive education, many who opposed the Hartmann arguments and/or inclusion were included in media coverage or wrote commentaries against the issue. Their oppositional narratives suggested the following themes:

Theme 1: Not in My Kid's School

This narrative presupposes that inclusive education will always have a disruptive effect on non-disabled children in the classroom and therefore should not be allowed. It is based on some anecdotal reports that a few severely disabled children, such as those with autism, have been disruptive. However, there is also much anecdotal evidence of disruptive non-disabled children, which is rarely mentioned in anti-inclusion narratives.

One parent, Steve Holladay, a university professor in Blacksburg, stated this narrative through his commentary piece in *The Roanoke Times*. Holladay claimed to quote his daughter, whose words were "shocking": "Many of these children (inclusion students) are uncontrollable. They enter your classroom in the middle of a class, and it may take 15 minutes for their aide to return them to the classroom they are assigned to. They break into loud crying fits or other noise-making episodes regularly, at unpredictable times and without apparent cause, bringing a halt to teaching until control is re-established. They wander around the class while the teacher is trying to teach, sometimes selecting a student to sit with and engage in an up-close, face-to-face staring contest. They may unexpectedly slap you in the forehead when you walk by them in the hall.... It cannot be denied that many of these children are extremely disruptive. And if they have been found to be too disruptive for normal classrooms in other school districts, why do we place them in our classrooms where our children have their only opportunity to learn many foundational concepts? Do they magically behave better here? ...Montgomery County has become an island that will accept highly disruptive children into our schools, children impaired to the point of being totally oblivious to the educational process going on around them. These children are incapable of learning in any way marginally related to the original intent of the school's programs, or to the expectations placed on other children in the classrooms" (Holladay, 1998, p. A7).

Other parents present this narrative of the disruptive effect of inclusive education. Even the mother of an autistic child wrote: "I am the mother of an autistic child, and I agree with Steve Holladay.... I do believe in mainstreaming, where the child is placed in a regular classroom for short periods of time and gradually works up to a full class period. With mainstreaming, 'normal' children get the education they deserve and need without disruption by our 'learning-challenged' children" (Kingery, 1998, p. A7).

Theme 2: Protect the Sensitive "Normal" Students

Those who question inclusion also argued that it may be traumatic for non-disabled children to be in the presence of severely disabled children: Beyond lost education, what effect might this have on the sensitive child who isn't yet ready to experience this type of behavior and instability?

"I am sincerely sympathetic for Ms. Hartmann and her situation, and very thankful that my own children are healthy. I further admire her obvious determination to provide what she believes to be the best growing and learning environment possible for her son. However, she and others who move here to take advantage of our inclusion policy seem to have little concern about the effect their children may have on other children in the classrooms....

"Does Ms. Hartmann care about the boy or girl who sits in front of the inclusion child during the uncontrollable screaming fit? What about the child whose personal space is invaded by stares or inappropriate touching? Or my own daughter, who receives a stunning slap on the forehead out of the blue? I asked other adults for their views about our inclusion policy. Not one spoke positively about it. One individual told of a girl whose earring was torn off by an inclusion child, and who subsequently was terrified of going to school. Another said her son quit Scouts because an inclusion child had selected him to shadow and touch" (Holladay, 1998, p. A7).

Theme 3: School is about Academics

In contrast with the inclusive education argument that it benefits children in many more ways than just academics, those opposed to the practice argue schools are to provide an education in reading, writing, arithmetic, etc. The attorney for Loudoun County illustrates this narrative in her comments to NPR's Morning Edition. Kathleen Mehfoud, Attorney for Loudoun County, Virginia Schools: "Socialization is part of that, but academic and educational instruction is obviously the primary responsibility. So, Loudoun would have had to totally overlook the educational requirements in favor of a minor goal" (Abramson & Chadwick, 1997b).

Holladay ties the idea of a proper learning environment with this narrative and argues that inclusive education is its antithesis. "Doesn't it seem obvious that loss of teaching time to disruptive or ongoing distractive behavior isn't conducive to learning? Similar to Ms. Hartmann, we (the other parents) are also determined to provide our children the best possible learning environment. As an educator myself, I don't like our inclusion policy. I would never tolerate such disruption in my classrooms unless, as has become the case in Montgomery County, I was mandated to do so by law. I truly do care about Mark. However, I care more about his classmates who can learn algebra and Spanish, children for whom the schools were intended, and whose futures will ultimately depend on what they learn now" (Holladay, 1998, p. A7).

Theme 4: Attendance is not the same as Integration

This narrative questions definitions of inclusive education. It also re-interprets various aspects of inclusive education as having a negative effect. For example, Richard Schattman, a Vermont principal who believes in inclusion, explains how inclusion, when poorly implemented, gives those opposed to inclusive education fodder to urge for its dismantling. "A student can be more isolated and segregated in a normal classroom than in special education," Mr. Schattman said. "Inclusion isn't about placing the kid. It's about making the placement successful both for the kid and for the rest of the class. And it's not easy. You need small classes, lots of planning time, and staff that believes in it." Some special education experts worry that the inclusion movement may lead to dumping children with special needs into classes where they will be ignored or taunted, and eliminating the special services and support that they receive in settings intended just for them (*Inclusive Education* 887).

"It has not been demonstrated that regular classrooms, even fortified regular classrooms using the best practices can accommodate all children all the time," said Douglas Fuchs, a professor of special education at Vanderbilt University. "The full inclusionists honestly believe that creating a situation in which teachers individualize instruction for each student is a terrific goal we should all dedicate our lives to. So we should kick away the crutch of special education. But that's a high stakes game, and I'm not sure it's realistic." Nor are all parents and advocates for children with disabilities convinced that it is the correct goal (Lewin, 1997, p. 20).

This narrative supports those opposed to inclusion by noting that it may not be the right accommodation for every disabled child. This type of theme turns inclusive education on itself, i.e., because it may not be appropriate for all disabled children, maybe it should not be used at all.

The New York Times story above continued the narrative by explaining that because of disruptive, abusive, and violent children,

Vermont, the premier state for successful inclusive education, is placing such children in separate settings (Lewin, 1997).

Conclusions and Discussion

As noted in this analysis, narrative themes were divided into those that support the Hartmanns/inclusive education and those that do not. This reflects a problem that is imbedded within the debate itself, by creating a division that oversimplifies the nature of inclusive education. The public discussion about this case reflects standard news coverage of a controversial issue, an "either–or" dichotomy, debate rather than discussion (Tannen, 1998). When the news narratives follow lines of "yes" or "no" about inclusive education, they miss an opportunity to critically assess the issue for all children in U.S. public school systems. When the focus is on a two-sided debate, rather than a multifaceted discussion, the news media are also more likely to drop coverage of the topic if one side of the debate tires of presenting their narratives.

The media stories and commentaries, and the themes they illustrate about inclusive education, lend insight into the participants' beliefs, actions and worldviews, as well as their conflicts of opinion and perception relative to the setting (Hollihan & Riley, 1987). Although this paper touched on just a few of the prominent themes about inclusive education in the news, we believe the themes offered in this paper dominate the discussion. Furthermore, we conclude that even though some parents of non-disabled children are vehemently opposed to inclusive education, it was the more numerous and more vocal parents of severely disabled children, educators, and proponents of IDEA who set the tone of the debate and framed inclusion as a workable approach to educate disabled children. We conclude that though the Hartmanns lost their case against Loudoun County, the narratives they inspired actually won in the court of public opinion.

It has taken almost twenty-five years for pro-inclusion narratives to take hold. As programs in Montgomery County, VA, Illinois, and Vermont show, school districts need not only well-trained faculty and well-financed programs to succeed, but public support as well. For example, when parent Steve Holladay wrote to criticize inclusive education in Montgomery County, his criticism was met with seven letters to the editor positively endorsing inclusive education. In the pro-inclusion environment of Montgomery County, the local newspaper, *The Roanoke Times*, seemed to present the proponents' narratives wholeheartedly. Even when the Hartmanns lost their case, the newspaper published a family provided color photo of Mark Hartmann on its front page (Lu, 1998). In the photo, Mark Hartmann, in a T-shirt and shorts, grins broadly as a picture-perfect "average" kid. The image alone provides a "good reason" that Mark should be in a regular classroom because he is presented visually as a "regular kid." Earlier, the newspaper published a large two-page spread on inclusive education in the county, providing a location for thoughtful discussion of the issue and primarily "good reasons" for inclusive education.

Some opponents of inclusive education fear the public and policymakers may be swayed by an underlying message of pity for the "poor, little disabled children." The conservative *National Journal* feared during the re-authorization of IDEA in 1997 that: Overhaul of the Individuals with Disabilities Education Act is tailor made for policy decision by anecdote. The facts and figures are sparse and conflicting; the horror stories are stark and vivid. And the interest groups are well organized, disciplined and loaded with heart tuggers or spine chillers, depending on their legislative goal. In the past, organizations representing the disabled could count on their substantial political clout in Congress. "Politicians are terrified of them—that they'll trot out people in wheelchairs," a lobbyist for an education organization said enviously. "It's very easy for a Member to feel virtuous voting for their issues" (Stanfield, 1995).

Yet, the findings from this narrative analysis illustrate that proponents of inclusive education have no need to trot out hackneyed, pity images of disabled children. They rely on much stronger and more salient narratives: inclusion is a win-win situation for everyone; public education is every child's right; inclusion is cheaper than institutionalization; and inclusion has proven itself successful nationally. These "good reasons" hold the most persuasive power because they appeal to the audience's general understanding of equality and humanity, which most Americans embrace.

As one woman with cerebral palsy and a hearing impairment explained the good reasons from her personal inclusion experience: Disabled "children are more likely to learn appropriate behavior if they are 'included' in regular classes. Able-bodied children learn about acceptance, tolerance and compassion toward those who are different, and perhaps something about 'the power of the human spirit.' Not all education is gained from books and facts" (Vass-Gal, 1998, p. A7).

These themes/stories in support of inclusion are consistent

with American values of equality—the country has determined that schools cannot be separate and truly equal. Furthermore, the effects of inclusion, while perhaps detrimental to a few students, largely have promising effects for both students with and without disabilities. Inclusion represents the notion of a powerful narrative being representative of an ideal basis for conduct.

While many of the stories against inclusion suggest pragmatic or traditional bases for educational policy, readers of the narratives are likely to find the rationality of the pro-inclusion arguments more consistent with U.S. history and culture. For example, the 1960s civil rights movement, which successfully dismantled separate, but unequal educational systems for blacks and whites, suggests the type of ideal conduct to which Fisher refers. The civil rights movement forced the United States to once again acknowledge the central narrative of its founding—that all citizens are created equal and deserve equal opportunities in all aspects of U.S. society, including education. Although the narratives evaluated in this study were only linked to the media coverage of inclusive education, we believe another area of inquiry could involve comparing coverage of this movement for disabled children with narratives reported in media about desegregation of US schools in the 1960s and 1970s. Would narratives from both movements support the same or similar themes? U.S. history tells us that some of the same arguments and cultural values were employed during that period of change in U.S. educational policy. For example, some of those who were against the integration of black children into predominantly white schools made some arguments parallel to those opposed to inclusion: that desegregation would be disturbing to both black and white children, that it would be disruptive to the academic process, that schools were for academics not socialization, and that some students were not served by desegregation. Our conclusion is that just as these anti-integration narratives proved less persuasive in the 1960s, the narratives against inclusion are becoming less effective today.

After the loss of her son's case, Roxana Hartmann said she will continue to lead national discourse about inclusive education: "This is the end, but it's not going to stop me from talking about inclusion," Roxana said. "No, if anything, it's made me more of a believer than ever.... This is not about winners and losers; this is about schools doing the right thing for children." (Lu, 1998, p. 1A).